GEORGE GROSZ

SERGE SABARSKY

GEORGE GROSZ
The Berlin Years

Contributions by
Marty Grosz, Achille Bonito Oliva, Lothar Fischer,
Uwe M. Schneede, and Marina Schneede-Sczesny

RIZZOLI
NEW YORK

First published in 1985 in the United States of America by
RIZZOLI INTERNATIONAL PUBLICATIONS, INC.
597 Fifth Avenue, New York, NY 10017

Documentation, research and production coordination:
Christa E. Hartmann, Renée Price, New York
Ilse Schweinsteiger, Munich

Translation: Christa E. Hartmann and Hanna Hannah

Cover Design: Marcus Ratliff, New York

Photography: Margaret Dwyer Becker; Dorothee Jordens-Meintker; Nathan Rabin; Bauhaus-Archiv, Berlin; The Estate of George Grosz, Princeton, NJ; Hamburger Kunsthalle; The Heckscher Museum, Huntington, NY; Bundesarchiv, Koblenz; Landesbildstelle, Berlin; Bildarchiv Dr. Martin Hürlimann; The Metropolitan Museum of Art, New York; The Museum of Modern Art, New York; Nationalgalerie Berlin; Staatsgalerie Stuttgart.

Production: Carlo Giani

Library of Congress Cataloging-in-Publication Data

Sabarsky, Serge.
    George Grosz : The Berlin Years.

    Bibliography: p.
    1. Grosz, George, 1893–1959—Views on politics.
2. Berlin (Germany)—Politics and government.
3. Berlin (Germany) in art.   I. Title
N6888.G742S2   1985   741'.092'4   85-24564
ISBN 0-8478-0668-5

Printed in Italy

CONTENTS

INTRODUCTION
Serge Sabarsky

For all his versatility—he was a draftsman, painter, costume and set designer, cofounder and advocate of new artistic schools, teacher, poet, writer, and political commentator—George Grosz emerges again and again as a supreme draftsman. He studied the art of drawing academically, but his consummate mastery of the technique was achieved through unending perseverance and practice. The thousands of drawings he produced in 1912 alone constitute an almost independent oeuvre by themselves. In his autobiography *A Little Yes and a Big No* Grosz records:

"I drew whatever I came across: household utensils, garden tools, kitchen equipment...I just kept at it, happily, blithely, and with never a cloud on my horizon.

. . .

Once, after reading about the famous Adolf von Menzel, I decided to do as he did and to make drawings wherever I happened to be or whatever I happened to be doing—standing, lying, sitting or dozing. Menzel's dictum—that diligence and industry were more important than talent—made a deep impression on me."

The typical "Grosz period" begins about 1915, and during this time Grosz accomplishes phenomenal works. He has already perfected his style to such an extent that it appears as if the eye itself guides his pen. His drawings from this period stand alone as precise renderings of the epoch and its people and need no written commentary to enhance them.

In the years to come, Grosz's acute sensitivity to the world enabled him to recreate it in his art with an accuracy that persistently aston-

7

ishes the viewer. Grosz recorded the things he was continually affected and enraged by. He was seeking justice yet he hated judges; he had compassion for mankind yet he ridiculed human nature. Thus he notes in his autobiography:

"I drew men drunk, men vomiting, men with clenched fists cursing the moon, men playing cards on the coffins of the women they had murdered. I drew wine drinkers, beer drinkers, schnapps drinkers and a frantic man washing the blood from his hands. I drew scenes of army life based on sketches I had made during my military service. I drew lonely little men rushing insanely through empty streets. I drew a cross-section of a tenement building: behind one window a man attacked his wife with a broom, behind another two people were making love, in a third a man was hanging from the crossbars of the window, surrounded by buzzing flies."

Otto Dix (1891–1969).

His colleague Otto Dix (1891–1969) draws and paints the countenance of the German people; George Grosz draws and paints the psyche. Both artists are advocates of truth who refuse to embellish it. Dix portrays and thus informs the audience, while Grosz's work incites to revolution. Dix depicts what he sees; Grosz—because of his analytic ability—looks behind society's mask and captures the essence of what he observes.

O. Dix, *Pregnant Woman*, 1920.

It would be a futile attempt to label George Grosz an expressionist, a New Realism painter, Dadaist, or metaphysician. It is also incorrect to dismiss him as a satirist and caricaturist. He is all of the foregoing and more. While Grosz indeed uses a style that caricatures, he employs it at the same time to expose banal, pompous, shamelessly exploitative, brutal, and perverse human beings. No other artist, not before or after Grosz, has succeeded so uniquely in capturing these types. The viewer is compelled to remember those close-minded, hypocritical bourgeois faces. Grosz heaps his mockery upon the profiteering industrialist, incompetent politicians, obtuse civil servants, and corrupt militarists as well as on any other imaginable representative of German society. Grosz's art is not only ridiculing, but also accusatory. He is enraged and furious at the injustice, narrow-mindedness, and deceiving impudence of those he portrays. Thus Grosz's contemporary, the author Kurt Tucholsky, comments in 1921:

O. Dix, *Harbor Scene*, 1922.

O. Dix, *Dead Guard*, 1924.

"I don't know of one who has been able to capture the modern face of the powerful down to the last red-wine capillaries as well as this one. He not only draws, but he exposes the figures—what patriotic mutton-legs! what paunches!—with their odors, their entire sphere of existence in their own world. The way in which Grosz depicts these officers, these industrialists, these public guardian's of law and order in each and every situation, that's the way they always are as long as they live."

In addition Grosz portrays his individuals so eloquently that they are recognizable without distinctive clues. This makes them even more effective. A judge drawn by Grosz, for instance, does not need his robe to be classified as a magistrate. Grosz's relentless depiction of the opressor is counterbalanced by his empathetic portrayal of the victim, a clear illustration of George Grosz's philanthropic nature.

Sometimes he put aside his penetrating pen and painted—as recreation, so to speak—rather opulent "beautiful" nudes or peaceful landscapes (for example, on his trips to France in 1927). He also often drew portraits of friends and famous people in Berlin, where in the twenties, tumultuous political events occurred. It was also a cultural center and fostered an experimentation in the arts. The theater was especially revolutionary, and Grosz designed costumes and/or sets for seven Berlin productions between 1919 and 1928. The prominent *Deutsche Theater* (German Theater) of director-producer Max Reinhardt remains even today the embodiment of great theater. Erwin Piscator and his political theater were influential as well. In 1928 Piscator presented a stage production of Jaroslav Hašek's novel *Die Abenteuer des braven Soldaten Schwejk* (*The Adventures of the Good Soldier Schwejk*) and commissioned Grosz for background projections and costume and stage designs. Of the approximately three hundred drawings Grosz completed for the play, seventeen were published during the same year in his portfolio *Hintergrund* (*Background*). The emerging German film industry, however, hardly utilized Grosz's talent and potential. He merely did some work for the filming of Gerhard Hauptmann's *Die Weber* (*The Weavers*)—even designing the titles for this silent film. This was the time the director Josef von Sternberg created one of the first German sound pictures *The Blue Angel* which featured Marlene Dietrich in her unforgettable role as Lola. Another famous stage and film celebrity of the period

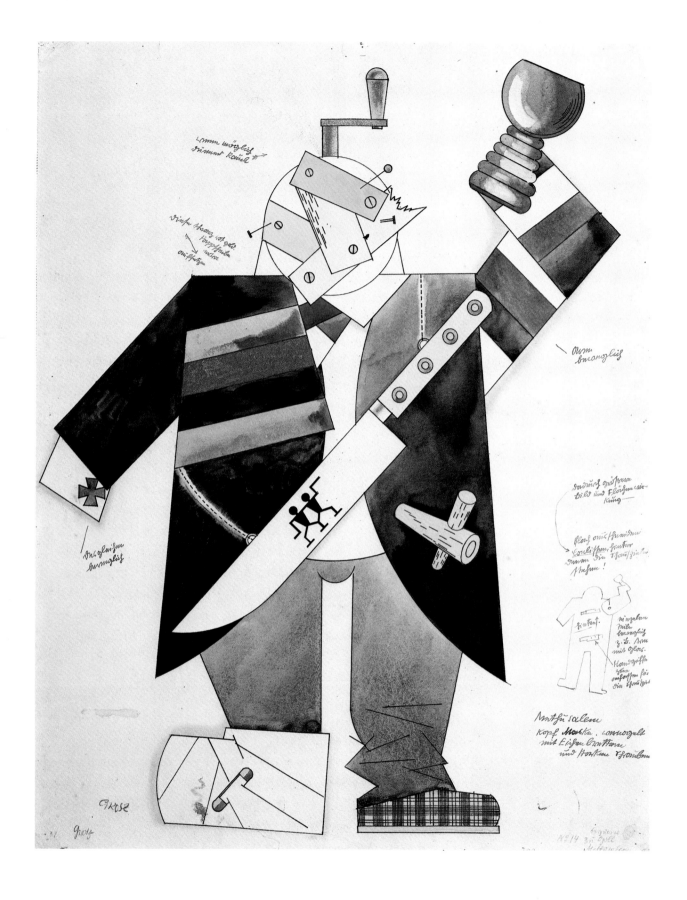

Marlene Dietrich in Joseph von Sternberg's *Blue Angel*, 1930.

Elisabeth Bergner in the film *Fräulein Else* after a play by Arthur Schnitzler.

was Elisabeth Bergner whose character performances remain forever memorable.

Above all, besides being a great artist and fighter for social justice, George Grosz was a chronicler. His works are a unique testimony to an entire era of German history. The fact that his prophetic drawings were not considered as such shows us the mentality of the German people of the time and makes the events subsequent to the twenties all the more understandable.

For this publication I have intentionally chosen the works created during Grosz's Berlin years since they not only delineate a geographical period in his life, but the years 1912 to 1932 also document specific artistic developments closely related to them. Moreover, after his emigration to America in 1933, a completely new creative phase commences, and George Grosz's accomplishments of these years deserve to be treated separately.

G. Grosz, *Methuselah*, 1922.
Pen and ink and watercolor,
52.6 × 41.1 cm.
The Museum of Modern Art,
New York.
Mr. and Mrs. Werner E. Josten
Fund.

George Grosz, 1927.

I REMEMBER...
Marty Grosz

George Grosz and Berlin. Berlin and George Grosz. For the period beginning with the First World War and ending with the Nazi take-over, the two are inseparable. I was only a fetus as the twenties were drawing to a close, and I was whisked away to America at the tender age of three, shortly after the Nazis burned the Reichstag.

Sometimes I could coax my father (I'll call him Grosz) to talk of those times, as when a gang of brownshirts hammered on his studio door bent upon exacting revenge upon the left-wing caricaturist whose acrid cartoons were exposing Hitler's thugs for what they were. Grosz answered the door clad in his work clothes, patched pants and a tattered shirt underneath a paint-smeared apron. Ever quick-witted, he assured his callers that he was only the janitor. Luckily the brownshirts believed him, and he escaped with his skin intact.

He would wince as my mother recounted his youthful impetuosities like the time he tossed a punchbowl out of the window during the course of someone's drunken party. The fenestration of the potables occurred because the other guests had become annoyed with his playing his favorite record, "Waiting for the Robert E. Lee," over and over. They wanted to dance to something slower. Grosz met their ill humor with his own fit of pique.

Once in America, Grosz, the incipient citizen, made a determined effort to put Europe behind him and to embrace his new homeland. Nevertheless, I was able to pry tales of the *Berliner Künstlerleben* out of him. Fellow painter Rudolf Schlichter, for instance, suffered from a foot fetish. To assuage his cravings he had a kind of harness constructed in his studio. He would bribe a prostitute to strap herself into the contraption which he then hoisted to the ceiling only to lower it slowly so he would worship his madonna as she descended.

Then there was Ringelnatz, the sailor poet, who would inveigle pert young ladies to his flat where they had to perch upon a steamer trunk in which the poet crouched like some feral animal ready to spring. After some moaning and meowing, he would burst forth from his prison, and, bellowing like a gored ox, chase the damsel, a satyr after a wood nymph, until she capitulated.

In later years when Grosz was besieged, as was often the case, by Philistines, poetasters, dilettantes, and epigones breathlessly praising him for his artistry, culture, and talent, he would brush their encomiums aside with the catchphrase, "Kunst ist Scheisse." The implications of these words had been concretely realized in Berlin by an acquaintance, a fellow painter, who actually laid a heavy impasto of excrement upon his canvasses.

George and Eva Grosz, Berlin 1920.

Not all of Grosz's reminiscences were of such a tawdry nature. He had loved Berlin, had embraced its gaiety, its spirit, its artistic ferment. But when he committed his Berlin to paper or canvas, it was with a moralist's hyper-critical eye. His pictures hung all over our home, and as a youngster, I took them quite literally. Here a Spiessburger's ear would be omitted, there an officer's arm would be redrawn several times giving the impression of a multiple-exposure snapshot. Buildings leaned threateningly as little and big people marched across his cityscapes without regard to perspective. Large-eyed women strolled boulevards or lounged in cafés in transparent clothing, to be leered at and fondled by men with dog tongues and pig snouts. Most of his males were endowed with an extra layer of neck fat which squeezed from the back of their celluloid collars.

After we settled on Long Island our home was constantly filled with friends from Berlin days: Wieland Herzfelde of the Malik Verlag and family; the Doctor Richard Hülsenbeck, he a former dada poet; the playwright Bert Brecht; the theater director Erwin Piscator; the philosopher-teacher Hermann Borchardt; and Hollywood screenwriter Ben Hecht, who met Grosz after World War I when Hecht was in Berlin reporting for the *Chicago Daily News*. None of these men had ears missing, dog tongues, pig snouts, or fat rolls at the neck. Nor was I able, try as I might, to see through their wives' or daughters' dresses.

George Grosz and Max Pechstein, ca. 1927.

Under mushrooms of cigar smoke, and accompanied by the clinking of whiskey-filled glasses, the expatriates would recall the Berlin which they had to flee because they were of an unwanted religious or political persuasion. Often Grosz entertained with songs and skits from the old days. He sang numbers such as "Wenn ich morgen denn den Feger mit dem Besen sehe und die Strassenbahn die geht Bim Bim," "Immer an der Wand lang," "Dass ist die Berliner Luft," and "Hab'n sie nicht den kleinen Cohn gesehen."

He recalled his debut as a Dada comedian. The high point of that performance occurred when he purposely tripped on a horseshoe which he then picked up and proceeded to eat; it was chocolate. He topped this dazzling turn by plucking a fellow actor's bow tie and gulping it down; it was licorice. Throughout the performance his fiancée stood on a ladder and doused the actors with buckets of water. All of this silliness outraged the audience, which is exactly what the players intended.

For Grosz, there never was a city that could take the place of Berlin with its six–day bicycle races, dinners at Kempinski, boxing matches, cocaine snorting, street fighting, disabled veterans begging on every corner, pimps and whores, and nightclubs which catered to every possible sexual proclivity.

In his last years he announced his intention of dividing his time between New York and Berlin. Much fuss was made over him by the Berlin city fathers. After his return there, some old cronies organized a welcome-home party in his honor. Beer and schnapps flowed. Old songs were intoned in voices made raspy by time. Couples tottered through the Charleston and Black Bottom. Skirts were raised and bottoms pinched while elderly coquettes winked and cooed. Alas, it was too late. The real party that was Berlin had moved on.

THE COMMON SENSE OF THE GROTESQUE

Achille Bonito Oliva

G. Grosz, *Self-Portrait*, 1917.

G. Grosz, *Republican Automatons*, 1920.
Pen and ink and watercolor,
60 × 47.3 cm.
The Museum of Modern Art,
New York.
Advisory Committee Fund.

"Man is beast," declared George Grosz, reversing the expressionist slogan which had pointed to the inherently good, but humiliated, nature of man, crushed under the logic of reason. The statement represents the political core of this German artist who had gradually shifted from a vital dadaist position to one sharply political after which he would never again delude himself about human nature in which he discerned an egoism reinforced by the brutality of money.

Nevertheless throughout the span of his life Grosz's narcissistic and individualistic anarchism as a dadaist was crossed with a political bent derived from Communist ideology and in particular its splinter group. Man, good or evil, required an art which would speak to him collectively, and if reproduced serially, would found a universal message capable of addressing everyone.

Such a universality was possible through the borrowing of a style, of influences from various sources both from the world of high culture and from the mass media such as comic strips, the thriller and serial novels. In this sense, Grosz had no scruples; as a true dadaist he had created works irreverently crossing different cultural climates, butting up against the underside of the explicit. Along with Hülsenbeck, Hausmann, Jung, Hannah Höch, Baader, Herzfelde, and Heartfield, he found himself at the inspirational fulcrum of Berlin Dada, in a position at the same time experimental and illustrative. Without the myth of art, Grosz posed himself the problem of art's role and its immediate effect. Because of this he could not lean too much on the side of a pure linguistic revolution and instead, quite naturally, he accompanied each work with a descriptive and didactic tension.

17

George Grosz, Berlin, 1920.

G. Grosz, *The Guilty One Remains Unknown*, 1919.

Formalism became an object against which to fight with the armies of art itself. To be at the avant-garde meant, to him, to outstrip the avant-garde itself, to transform the objective search for a new language in a directed and biased exploitation of language. Drawing became the means through which to exalt an objective and impersonalized content.

The impersonal was the ethical character of his work, capable of toning down those elements of originality which would sometimes touch upon his private though hardly dull or gray life. His eccentricity, typically dada, became the distinctive characteristic of that existentialist element which had been removed from the graphic work.

Grosz buried his dandyism, the individualism of another era, when it came to his work, accentuating the impersonal which, in his view, reflected the times.

"Line has become a photographic and not a personal fact," Grosz upheld. Photography, by definition, objectifies the features of the subject and renders them legible as external objects; it strips the sign from any autobiographical substance by placing it at the same level of realistic appearances. The paradox is this: to alter a language spawned from the ideology within a condition of ineluctability and necessity is the only possible transposition in an alienated universe.

The mechanical means of photography assimilate, onto the same grid, the indeterminate coordinates of twentieth-century man, the man of the masses characterized by structural elements of similarity rather than dissimilarity. The artist became the means to such an assimilation which he realized through the devaluation of the image and the stereotyped signs, as in the work of a perverse designer who insists on using expressive material in only one persistent way, even in the face of the indifferent masses.

Asymmetry, multiple views and erotic obscenity became the connotations of an anthropomorphic image which reflected Grosz's sarcasm evoking man only from the point of view of the deformed, the grotesque, through satyric caricature typical of the popular newspapers. The mark, as a sign of protest at the edge of graffiti, does not lend itself to cosmetic superstructures, but only to a purifying reductiveness.

On the other hand, the repressive nature of a certain dadaist primitivism helped Grosz, in this bare-bones reductiveness, to arrive at the essential by taking a direct shortcut with the use of grotesque cartoons. These seemed to be the most advanced product of a mass society of infantile and American taste in the extreme. But the childishness of the mark was not a symptom of reduction, but rather an anarchistic decision which pushed the German artist to go beyond the mere hedonism of a beautiful creation.

If "man is beast," as he upheld, then it was necessary to bestialize the work, to push it toward a disgust with harmonious proportions and beautiful symmetry, and toward contradiction and eclecticism. Like a designer who copies given popular situations, Grosz simply transferred outright the styles of the avant garde, Expressionism and Cubism with carbon paper which reproduced, through this process, only the most schematic lines, eliminating the more complex and abstruse ones.

G. Grosz, *Dada* illustration, 1918.

In fact, the idea and the representation of space verged on the amorphous and the deformed, floating laterally like a flight without depth, on which the smug face of bestial man—always the bourgeois—inscribes itself.

The simplicity of the human figure, at the limits of a didactic poetics of the grotesque, inhabits a space sometimes articulated with marks borrowed from a modern and experimental language. The primitive beast broods within a highly structured visual ground.

This is the result of a schism which genuinely informs Grosz's work: the adult decision to imitate an obscene child. On the other hand, he identified blindly with his ideological vision, studying, in an almost scientific way, the manifestations of an infantile universe: the graffiti on bathroom walls that belongs to a certain class such as the proletariat which through word and image expresses its own exasperation and anger.

Grosz's "cutting style" was the result of an exercise which literally cut away all allusion in favor of the explicit, the implicit in favor of (outright) denunciation. The clumsiness of a child's or a primitive's drawing was part of the avant garde culture of the time—dadaist or cubist—when the anthropological universe of the primitive world and its linguistic value was rediscovered through these very same movements.

All of this was a direct source for his ideological work, with its

G. Grosz, *Daum Marries her Pedantic Automaton George, John Heartfield is Very Glad of It*, 1920.

programmed lack of love; and this adherence under the pressure of his commitment caused him to rework several styles.

The transgressive language of sex, basically figurative, was repressed and altered in an emphatic manner—hidden in a spatially theatrical frame, with background and wings which set in relief the obscene scenario.

Grosz's stylistic dissociation was programmatic and always realized with a dadaist penchant for the mistrust of coherence. "Coherence is for those who do not have ideas" (Feyerabend). The German artist, however, was armed with ideas and voluntarily bereft of a respectable sense of coherence. A subtle kind of hypocrisy governed his compositions in that they were patterned after the obscene images of popular culture but boxed into a twistedly-constructed space typical of the sophisticated culture of the avant-garde.

Basically society at that time had no coherence and went about confronted by its own weapons—those of the imitation of bad taste, those of the mask and the yell, vulgarity and its double meaning, the singular and schematic rendering of the amicable grimace of tyranny. Grosz set about to make images which would overwhelm the spectator and assault the fine palate of the public.

He set forth the characteristics of his time, like a distorting mirror which never functions on realistic terms or exact duplication. In the universe inhabited by bestial men one does not feel pressured.

In this universe a rational order cannot exist naturally where an uprooted sense of space decomposes the picture plane, sloping and wrapping itself around the sinful protagonists.

The collapse of space and its objects was not an expression of implicit eroticism but rather of "the lack of love," as Grosz himself put it, in so far as it was a symptom of a loveless crowd which was ready to do itself in. The dominating structure takes place within and without the subject in tune with the social struggle. Grosz himself consisted of a superimposition of many personalities quarrelling among themselves in fantastical and literary terms in a typically psychoanalytical tension.

In this sense all of Grosz's work was a visual diagram of a real situation preventing us from seeing his images as a mere distortion of a symmetrical and orderly model. Rather the distoriton was observed to exist at the core of things and people and therefore, within the figures and objects depicted and arranged, with a programmatic eye, at the edge of a metaphysic.

A common sense of the grotesque continues to inhabit the imagination of this German artist who by now has arrived at a kind of anthropological documentation which feigns indifference toward the entomologist and transmits the penetrating vision which strips each event of its hypocrisy to consign it to its essential nudity as schematic paradigm.

Grosz's visual paradigm challenges the inevitability of repetition typical of a mechanical universe while at the same time choosing the role of ideological designer who now decides he wants to show the impossibility of change, and thus, produces a pleasant surprise.

GEORGE GROSZ—THE ROOTS OF HIS ART

Lothar Fischer

The life of any artist is naturally affected by certain decisive years, those periods during which the ideas grow and develop that later take definite forms and visible shapes in his work. What were these formative influences in the case of George Grosz?

After a happy childhood in Stolp, Pomerania, Grosz's father dies, and his mother takes the family to Berlin. The new home is close to the Wedding district—the proletarian section on the north side of town—opposite a coal yard. The company's sign—two crossed black hammers—represented to Grosz "a symbol of gloom. The tarred wall gave on to a back yard, the usual grey city backdrop of asphalt and stone." During those years Grosz gained his first insight into the grayness and hopelessness of proletarian life in a large city. The poverty of the working class as well as the desolate and gloomy streets evoked in him a certain pessimistic attitude toward the city.

Conflicts with his classmates in school make him reach the conclusion that mankind is evil, a feeling Grosz would reiterate in years to come. One day a schoolmate punches him in the back; he falls flat on his face and on the sandwich he is eating. Grosz recalled the episode in his autobiography: "Oddly enough, I have never forgotten that first incident, often reliving the surge of anger, the loneliness and the forlornness I experienced in that schoolyard. I have since come across the same type of individual in all walks of life; it was as if I had discovered a deeper law of brutality, and with it the ubiquitous urge people have to laugh at the misfortune of others."

Grosz emerged from his early school years as a rebel. He had retaliated when a teacher boxed him on the ear, and, to his mother's dismay, he was expelled from school. However, with the help of a

George Grosz, Berlin, 1920.

Kranzler-Ecke, intersection of Friedrichstrasse and Unter den Linden, Berlin ca. 1900.

local art teacher who had recognized Grosz's talent, he starts his training at the Dresden Academy of Fine Art. The traditional instructions at the academy are aimed at developing a meticulous and exact form of draftsmanship. He resents the academy's curriculum, but remains a student until 1911. During that time the artists of the Expressionist group Die Brücke are painting in Dresden. Although Grosz does not join them, he nevertheless is very excited about their new and diverse uses of color.

In 1912 Grosz settles in Berlin. With his friend and fellow student the painter Erich Fiedler from Leipzig he shared a cheap apartment in the suburb of Südende. The young artists, who remained lifelong friends, drew their surroundings. On the outskirts of a fast-growing and constantly changing city, they were able to sketch bizarre city landscapes, refuse dumps, newly erected buildings, allotment shacks—the "mansions" of the poor—fairgrounds with colorful caravans, show booths, circus tents, and the like. Grosz was fascinated by amusement parks and the circus. He particularily loved clowns. He saw them as playing the same tragicomic role that the artist was

25

forced to enact in a bourgeois society. The meeting place of the artist world in Berlin was the coffeehouse Café des Westens. During 1912 Grosz frequented the café with his face powdered white, wearing red lipstick, dressed in a padded checked jacket, and carrying a black cane with an ivory skull for a handle. Nobody recognized this stranger who came in regularly and usually sat at the edge of the terrace staring at the passersby and industriously filling notebooks with his sketches.

Grosz uses his art of the early Berlin years to attack the self-contentedness and self-righteousness of bourgeois society, primarily its plutocrats, during the German Empire. He anticipates far in advance the disillusionment and shock of World War One as well as the change in art and society brought about by the chaos of 1918. Grosz portrays the city from the perspective of a street-smart kid. Sneeringly he exposes the hypocrisy and underlying meanness of mankind. The sexual explicitness in his drawings matches the perverted knowledge of a precocious youth. Yet there are shades of humility and of longing for a better world evident in his works; despite his distaste for anything romantic, one cannot fail to notice rather poetic moons and stars shining above city streets. His old friend Fritz Harig told me once that Grosz was actually a grown-up child. He liked hurdy-gurdy music; it moved him to tears. This music represented to him the soul of old Berlin, the city he loved so dearly.

In 1913 Grosz lives for nine months in Paris and meets the painter Jules Pascin, whose works greatly impress him. The outbreak of World War One, however, interrupts their friendship.

As did so many intellectuals, Grosz enters military service in 1914 as a volunteer. After six months he is dismissed due to a severe sinus infection. In January 1917 Grosz is called up again and in May is discharged as permanently unfit for service. In his autobiography Grosz states that he was accused of desertion, but saved from execution by the intervention of his aristocratic patron, the art collector Count Harry Kessler. Yet, there are no records that mention either Grosz's desertion or the count's mediation.

Grosz returns to Berlin even more convinced of society's insanity. In 1918, together with John Heartfield, master of the political photomontage, and his brother Wieland Herzfelde, Grosz produces a cartoon film which unfortunately is lost today. They had been commissioned to make a war-propaganda film for Germany; instead, they turned it into its opposite. The brothers Heartfield/Herzfelde from now on help Grosz to become better known. Owning a small printing press enables them to untiringly publicize Grosz's works in books, journals, and exhibitions. Grosz also joins the November Group, a revolutionary organization of artists. In addition he becomes a leading member of the Berlin Dada movement. Although his own simple style is a precursor of Dada, Grosz discovers additional possibilities of expression through the new techniques of collage and happenings.

The growing power of the National Socialists could not fail to influence the position of George Grosz and his art. Despite being the most popular book illustrator of the late twenties, Grosz senses the impending doom and takes precautions. In 1932 he accepts an appointment as guest lecturer at the Art Students League in New York City and in 1933 he emigrates to the United States with his entire family. Only in 1959, after twenty-seven years of exile, does he return to his birthplace, Berlin. As if he had come full circle, George Grosz dies shortly afterward on July 6, 1959.

For generations to come, George Grosz will most certainly be one of the greatest German artists of the twentieth century. His vitriolic style as well as the contents of his works illustrate a social and psychological reality that painfully questions again and again our moral standards and the nature of human relations.

George Grosz in his studio, 1928.

INFERNAL APPARITIONS OF REALITY

Uwe M. Schneede

Reichstag building and Bismarck monument, Berlin.

New York, Hotel Waldorf-Astoria, June 1958. Theodor Heuss, president of the Federal Republic of Germany, sponsors a reception for emigrants and refugees who left Germany during the regime of the National Socialists. Many came, and among them is one who wanders about, looks closely at the president, but does not get in line to shake hands. He has been an American citizen for twenty years: George Grosz. Although he no longer considers himself a German, Grosz was unable to resist the invitation. For twenty-six years the sixty-five-year-old Grosz had lived in the New World, but yet it was not his home: he represents a German destiny caught between the Spree and Hudson rivers.

His Protestant and Prussian-militaristic upbringing in the era of Wilhelm II (1859–1941, emperor of Germany 1888–1918) fostered a longing for a different life, a life that he found in books. Robinson Crusoe and Karl May's Old Shatterhand were Grosz's heroes. Much of his youthful thinking was devoted to dreaming of America and romanticizing about a world of "dangers and bloody adventures." As early as 1916 he spoke of emigration, and in 1927 he wrote: "I shall leave Germany for a time." Five years later he arrived in New York City as guest lecturer, "not as a dissatisfied emigrant . . . not for political considerations. I rather went for economic reasons—mixed with a love for travel and adventure."

Grosz, who had been a much disputed but primarily celebrated artist in the Weimar Republic, felt like a "king without a country" in America. But his optimism prevailed: "Boy, what a world!!!! Here I will have the chance of a lifetime." New York, not Berlin, now became "the most beautiful city in the world." In 1935 he wrote very

29

proudly to the German theater producer-director Erwin Piscator: "We Americans..." By that time he was no longer voluntarily in the United States, as the National Socialists in Germany had outlawed his work and labeled it "degenerate."

The struggle of adapting to a life in exile along with the difficulties in establishing a new artistic career soon ended Grosz's enthusiasm for America; he tired of teaching "society girls" and he was unable to find an audience ("I am solely painting for myself"). In a letter to his brother-in-law Otto Schmalhausen he explained: "I play the part of the famous artist, but behind my fame looms a large hole." In the thirties his earlier optimism turned to despair. Grosz admitted that he "suffered from deep depressions, doubts and bouts of drunkenness." Yet, even after the war, it was not easy for him—the American—to return to Germany. Only in 1959 did he decide to live in Berlin again, but after six weeks he died, shortly before his sixtysixth birthday.

In 1912, after an early period of illustrative drawings that was still influenced by art nouveau, Grosz begins to sketch the world around him as he sees it. In addition Grosz is an avid reader, hence he also draws many scenes inspired by literature. His interest in adventure novels and police reports is particularly evident in his work. Grosz admits in his autobiography: "It was the strange, the mysterious, the often deliberately bizarre which fascinated me. With all my innate liking for the fantastic and the grotesquely satirical I still had a strong developed sense of reality."

About 1913 the subject of sex murders becomes one of his predominant themes. It reflects Grosz's inner rebellion against the Prussian mentality of law and order. By identifying with the criminal, the twenty-year-old Grosz revolts against society's status quo. Stylistically he is influenced by Alfred Kubin (1877–1959) as well as by Jules Pascin (1885–1930) whom he had met in Paris. In the late twenties Pascin's influence is even more evident in Grosz's drawings.

The most crucial event in Grosz's life was—as for most artists of his generation—World War One. The war experience radically changed him and his art. In 1914 Grosz volunteers for military service, an act that was quite common among intellectuals at that time. In May 1915 he is discharged as "unfit," but in January 1917 he is called up again. Thereupon he writes to his brother-in-law:

"My nerves went to pieces, this time even before I saw the front, decomposed corpses and barbed wire. My nerves, every fiber, disgust, revulsion!" And when he is admitted to a military hospital: "I am, God knows, no longer cheerful, my hatred of men has assumed monstrous dimensions. I'm walking through sheer hell." Grosz has to spend two months in a mental hospital. In April 1917 he is sent home and in May he is dismissed from the army, permanently unfit for service.

· Following his discharge Grosz creates paintings, watercolors, and drawings that show formal influences of Futurism. With regard to content, they depict modern city life with its desires, passions, and crimes. For Grosz, the chaos of the big city reflects the amorality of man. His basic attitude is totally pessimistic. By disregarding the laws of perspective, Grosz's drawings represent a world falling to pieces. In a letter to Otto Schmalhausen he explains that he demands "nothing more from men in a positive way, that's precisely why I fail to be sentimentally moved by so much rubbish, human shit, narrow-mindedness and superficial carrying-on!—on the contrary, the more the cesspool is stirred up, the better it pleases me—dear Oz! Do nail a motto over your bloody bed, once and for all; from the day they are confirmed to the day they are bumped off into the heavenly hustle and bustle beyond: 'Men are pigs.' "

After the war Grosz joins the Dadaists in Berlin. At first Dada engages in polemics against all traditional art forms and, by means of nonsense actions, tries to startle the bourgeoisie. But before long, shaped by the author and publisher Wieland Herzfelde, the writer Franz Jung, the artists John Heartfield and Rudolf Schlichter, Dada develops political characteristics. During the historic events of 1918–19, when it was yet undecided whether Germany would be headed by a socialist republic or parliamentary democratic government, the Berlin Dadaists side with the revolution. Most of them, including George Grosz, join the German Communist party. The producer-director Edwin Piscator, who was a member as well, recalls: "We had many discussions about art but solely with regard to politics. And we came to the conclusion that art, if it be worthwhile at all, must be committed to serve the class-struggle."

From that point on Grosz is very angry. He attacks those who schemed and made a profit from the war. He is indignant at those

31

who continue to support militarism after World War One during the First German Republic, and he is resentful of those who block all attempts at reform and democracy. Grosz is no longer interested in entertaining with his art, not even in a sarcastic sense. The purpose of his art is to fight, to influence, and to hurt: "My art . . . was to be a gun and a sword."

Using pointed pen strokes, unique contour lines, and strong over-statements, Grosz's penetrating drawings depict the militarists, the *nouveau riche* war profiteers, the degenerate bourgeoisie, and the lower middle classes. In a series of portfolios, Grosz combines his mastery of drawing techniques with caustic satire to provide a sociological record of those who would eventually destroy the Weimar Republic.

Grosz had to consider how his rebellious drawings would reach the public, since effectiveness of one's ideas depends on their distribution. Grosz's art would have been a useless tool without Wieland Herzfelde, the founder and owner of Malik-Verlag, a publishing house. Between 1918 and 1923 the bulk of Grosz's published work is done with Herzfelde. In addition many of his drawings appear in leftist journals. These publications—his illustrations, portfolios, books of drawings, and so forth—establish his reputation as a brilliant draftsman and probing observer of the German bourgeoisie. The contemporary author Kurt Tucholsky writes in 1920: "His portfolio *Gott mit uns* (*God With Us*) should not be missed from any middle class coffee-table—his caricatures of the faces of majors and sergeants are infernal apparitions of reality."

Grosz's accurateness in depicting the prevailing situation in Germany is evidenced in the authorities' reaction. In 1920 he is fined for attacking German soldiers and officers in his portfolio *Gott mit uns*. Kurt Tucholsky comments appropriately: "It is not the mirror's fault if it shows the virgin that she is pregnant." In 1924 Grosz is fined again for allegedly publishing obscene material in his portfolio *Ecce Homo*. In addition three drawings from his portfolio *Hinter-grund* (*Background*), which link German clergymen with militarism, cause one of the biggest uproars. Grosz is charged with having committed blasphemy against the church, and his trial lasts from 1928 to 1931. It is finally decided that one of the incriminatory drawings, *Christ With a Gas Mask*, is to be destroyed. But there is not much left to destroy since Grosz's publisher, Wieland Herzfelde, has sold all the prints, although they have been sealed by the police.

Just as the state charges Grosz with insulting the army, with damaging public morals, and with blasphemy, so does the dogmatic Left of the twenties attack Grosz for resigning as a member of the German Communist party. After a disappointing trip to the Soviet Union in 1923, he has become disillusioned with communism. As a result the leftists accuse him of turning from a fighter in the class struggle into a moralist, even into a painter of the *Neue Sachlichkeit* (New Realism) movement. More and more Grosz straddles the political fence.

But whoever wants Grosz to be consistent will necessarily miss all the contradictions of the man and his work. A cynic with lower middle class origins, striving to leave his inadequate social surroundings behind, Grosz attacked capitalism while always playing the role of the dandy himself. He unmasked the others, yet disguised himself by using aliases such as Lord Hatton Dixon, Dr. William King Thomas, or Count Ortyren-Bessler. He cursed the art world; nonetheless, he painted, at his dealer's suggestion, "saleable" landscapes without "offensive subjects," as he used to call them. In America he rejected his earlier political work, but continued to create political and antifascist drawings. These are the contradictions of a man who used his art to persecute narrowmindedness and brutality, and yet always remained haunted himself. He was haunted—or as he used to say "gehaunted"—first by the bourgeoisie, then by the courts, afterward by the National Socialists, and finally by his own past. In addition he was denounced by the Left, which had once relied upon his support.

In his autobiography Grosz confesses: "I did my utmost to emulate Walt Whitman, who once wrote: 'Do I contradict myself? / Very well then I contradict myself. / (I am large, I contain multitudes.)' " Everything he paints, draws, and writes is characterized by these "multitudes" and contradictions; indeed, Grosz's work actually develops out of this challenge. The shattering experiences of World War One, the destroyed hopes after the failed revolution of 1918–19, the resignation at the return of the old order in the Weimar Republic that was followed by the rise of fascism, and finally, the anomie created by exile, are all reflected in his oeuvre. The contradictions of such tumultuous and shocking events were not resolved by Grosz's work; on the contrary, his art only accentuated them.

*

In essays and statements Grosz defended himself against being considered an artist in the traditional sense: "For me art is not a matter of aesthetics. ...no musical scribbling to be responded to or fathomed only by the sensitive educated few. Drawing once more must subordinate itself to a social purpose." His attacks were chiefly directed against the French "beautiful art of painting." Grosz was mainly influenced by the late medieval German social satires found in pamphlets. He wanted to be known as a journalist whose medium is drawing, and he wished to exert a reforming influence on as many people as possible. Thus he preferred to publish his work in popular leftist journals rather than art magazines, and for the same reason he accepted the lowest possible fees for his drawings published by Wieland Herzfelde's press, Malik-Verlag.

Today we may realize that Grosz's drawings go far beyond common cartoons. His satire was not rooted in humor; it was, rather, devastatingly serious. His works are distinctive inasmuch as they break new aesthetic ground while opposing pictorial conventions and lacking any need to entertain. Grosz drawings that have no political or social overtones are almost unthinkable, but their true effectiveness (and they are certainly still strong today) results from his unique drawing technique. It is this technique that separates his drawings from the cartoons of the daily press and classifies them as belonging to the great tradition of art that provides an uncompromising critique of the period.

The failure of his work to prevent the rise of National Socialism, the party's ascent to power, and the dreadful events that ensued embittered Grosz in the late twenties and thirties and finally changed the course of his life. From that point his anger was directed at the futility of his involvement, but not at the committment itself. In 1913 he wrote to his friend Wieland Herzfelde: "There can be no doubt that my drawings were some of the strongest public statements against a certain German brutality. Today they are truer than ever—one day, in a more 'humane' period, one will exhibit them as one does now with Goya's pictures."

Goya's and Grosz's works share a similarity as documents that express political astuteness and courageous individual protest against social injustice. Grosz saw the cause for the political collapse in the continuance of the Prussian militaristic thinking. Today this view is undisputed. Both Grosz and Goya created artworks of the highest order: graphic masterpieces, unique for their period. The singular way in which Grosz combined political awareness, moral responsibility, and artistic precision in his work has yet to be equaled.

HISTORICAL DOCUMENTARY OF GROSZ'S GERMANY
Compiled by Marina Schneede-Sczesny

Wilhelm II in full-dress uniform

Wilhelm II (1859–1941), emperor of Germany from 1888 to 1918, was the chief proponent of Germany as a world power. In his empire, the emphasis was on raising patriots rather than citizens.

One of the most important holidays was Sedan-Day, the day on which, in 1870, Napoleon III capitulated to the Germans. Celebrated as the true day of the birth of the second German Empire, it was a constant provocation of neighboring France.

In the German Empire, the outbreak of World War I aroused rejoicing. On August 1, 1914 Wilhelm II announced from the balcony of the *Berliner Schloss:* "I no longer know any political parties, I know only Germans."

On August 2, 1914 Germany mobilized; on August 3 she declared war on France. On August 4 the German Reichstag unanimously approved the war credits. The parties abstained from political debates. However, within the German Socialist Party (SPD), opposition to the approval of war loans steadily became louder. Unequivocally opposed were Karl Liebknecht, Rosa Luxemburg, Clara Zetkin, and others.

Start of World War I, August 1914

Wounded soldiers of World War I

In the battle of Tannenberg in East Prussia (August 23 to 31, 1914) Hindenburg, with Ludendorff as his Chief of Staff, defeated the Russian army. Tannenberg was the only battle of annihilation of World War I. It established Hindenburg's fame in Germany.

Ludendorff, one of the theoreticians of German militarism, saw war as the supreme manifestation of the national will to live. For him the function of politics was to serve warfare. "Sound politics are a continuation of war in peacetime, simply using different means"—a brand of militarism which was to become the basis for Hitler's actions.

German patrol during a poison gas attack, 1915

Feeding the German population from public war kitchens during World War I

Women in a shell factory, 1916

On August 29, 1916, Wilhelm II appointed Hindenburg and Luddendorff to head the Supreme Command of the army. They supported the theory of "total war", i.e. not merely to wear the enemy out, but to annihilate him. On August 31, 1916, what was known as the Hindenburg Program was drawn up, demanding the doubling of munitions production and the trebling of production of cannon and machine guns by spring 1917.

The Hindenburg Program—notwithstanding harsh strong-arm measures—failed to reach its targets. The consequence of this hard line was an increase in destitution in the country. Because of the Allied naval blockade, the food situation deteriorated disastrously during the winter of 1916–17. The weekly rations for adults were: 1900g. bread, 2500g. potatoes, 80g. butter, 250g. meat, 180g. sugar. To make things worse, the potato crop of 1916 failed so that turnips became the staple food of the workers. Lack of coal made the "winter of the turnips" even worse. During the years 1914 to 1918, more than three quarters of a million people died of starvation.

After the men had been called up, the women became the providers. As they were forced to do even the heaviest physical work, the percentage of women working in the metal industry, for instance, rose from 6.6% in 1914 to 32.5% in the following year. Female labor yielded particularly high profits because women were paid not even half the wages for the same work previously done by men.

Spartacists in street fighting, Berlin, November 1918

On October 28, 1918, when the war was already lost, the German naval command nevertheless planned yet another attack against England: the result was a mutiny in the Navy. On November 3 at a mass demonstration workers and soldiers at Kiel declared their solidarity with the seamen. Among their demands were the immediate termination of the war, the release of arrested seamen and all political prisoners, freedom of the press and speech, and universal democratic suffrage. In the days that followed, workers' and soldiers' councils were formed in many big cities of the Reich: this was the November Revolution. On November 9 the emperor, Wilhelm II, abdicated. Friedrich Ebert, president of the German Socialist Party (SPD), became Chancellor of the Reich and Philipp Scheidemann (SPD) proclaimed the German Republic. On the same day Karl Liebknecht proclaimed the Socialist Republic, demanding the immediate drastic reform of the army, expropriation of all funds owned by banks of the mines and the steel industry, considerably shorter working hours, and the fixing of minimum wages. He called on the workers to fight until they had achieved their goal, a government of workers and soldiers, "the creation of a new national order of the proletariat."

On November 10, 1918 the government of the "Council of the Representatives of the People" was formed from three members each of the German Socialist Party (SPD) and the Independent Social Democratic Party of Germany (USPD). In addition there was the "Executive Council of Workers' and Soldiers' Councils." At that moment the council system and parliamentary democracy were equally under discussion.

Karl Liebknecht during an address in Berlin, December 1918

Funeral of victims of the December riots in Berlin, 1918

Government troops shielded by a tank, Berlin, March 1919

As early as the autumn of 1914 a group, which from January 1916 on calls itself "Spartacus," detached itself from the German Socialist Party (SPD). Under the leadershlip of Karl Liebknecht and Rosa Luxemburg, Spartacus rejected any support of Germany's war politics. Spartacus saw its main task in the "international class struggle against the war in order to enforce peace through the will of the masses."

On November 11, 1918, the Spartacus League was founded, comprising all Spartacus supporters in Germany. On December 31, 1918 the Spartacus League formed the Communist Party of Germany (KPD).

A Reichswehr soldier follows a worker, Berlin, March 1919

Spartacus revolt, Spartacists in front of the Mosse building, Berlin, January 1919

Potsdamer Platz in Berlin during electioneering for the National Assembly elections on January 19, 1919

Kapp Putsch, Berlin, March 14, 1920: first attack upon democracy

On January 5, 1919, after a demonstration, workers occupied the publishing houses of Ullstein, Mosse and Scherl, the Social Democratic newspaper *Vorwärts* (*Forward*), as well as railway stations and the printing works of the Reich. On January 6 the Revolutionary Committee decided to call a general strike. Between January 6 and 15 the revolt was brutally crushed by troops consisting mainly of anti-republican Free Corps companies of the High Command under the supreme command of the people's representative, Gustav Noske (SPD).

Karl Liebknecht and Rosa Luxemburg were arrested on January 15, 1919 and murdered.

The elections for a National Assembly took place on January 19, 1919. For the first time in Germany, women were allowed to vote. The SPD emerged from the elections as the strongest party. On Febrary 11, 1919 the National Assembly in Weimar elected SPD Chairman Friedrich Ebert as President of the Reich.

At the beginning of 1919 the workers were alarmed by the government's procrastination in implementing the socialization pro-

Electioneering by the SPD for the National Assembly in Berlin on January 19, 1919

40

Rosa Luxemburg (1870-1919)

Inflation: children collecting pieces of coal dropped from the back of a truck

Inflation: starving Berliners outside a municipal kitchen for the poor, 1922

gram. In mid-February a considerable strike movement had started in the region of the Ruhr which, by February 20, numbered some 180,000 workers. Members of the Free Corps, security police, and civic guards were called in against the strikers. The Workers' Council of Greater Berlin decided to call a general strike on March 1. Between March 2 and March 8 there were bloody clashes with a total of 1,200 deaths.

It was as early as the end of 1918, as the returning troops were welcomed as heroes, that the legend of the stab in the back began to circulate, poisoning the political climate of the Weimar Republic. It was the view expressed by the political Right that in World War I, the German Army would have been invincible but for the alleged revolutionary propaganda of the Social Democrats which had led to the demoralization of the front.

According to the terms of the peace treaty of Versailles, the German army had to be reduced to 100,000 men. Before long there was open resistance against the government, since the Free Corps and units of the Reichswehr (defensive forces) were equally threatened by these measures. On March 13, 1920, the long-planned coup of the radical Right took place. They occupied government buildings in Berlin and appointed Wolfgang Kapp, an East Prussian admin-

41

Right-wing extremist guerillas searching a cyclist for arms, 1923

Hitler (top left) at the Party Day ("Parteitag") of the NSDAP in Weimar, 1926

The President of the Reich Hindenburg and Field Marshal Mackensen, symbols of military power, July 1927

Demonstration of unemployed workers in favor of the referendum for the disinheritance of princes, 1926

istrator, as Chancellor of the Reich. However, members of the coup, which came to be known as the *Kapp-Putsch*, failed to gain the support even of the parties of the Right. The unions declared a general strike in which twelve million factory and office workers joined. The *Kapp-Putsch* collapsed after four days and Kapp fled to Sweden.

Almost nine tenths of the 160,000 million marks required for the conduct of the war had been raised by a total of nine war loans; this was the government's way of making inroads on the savings accounts of the middle classes. After Germany's defeat the excessive demands for reparations imposed on her by the Treaty of Versailles and the consequent overburdening of the economy resulted in a distinct lack of readiness on the part of the government to proceed with the repayment of these loans. What was left in middle-class savings accounts finally vanished after the war when the increased printing of paper money resulted in a rapidly escalating devaluation, or inflation.

Ludendorff and Hitler after Hitler's trial, March 1924

This devaluation was accelerated after the war by a flight of capital, foreign currency speculation and what was known as "flight into material assets," resulting in a far-reaching shift in the distribution of wealth and income. Those who had least lost most: the real wages of workers decreased because wages were constantly lagging behind price rises, while wage increases had to be fought for afterwards. The dwindling purchasing power of money led to an indescribable shortage of essential goods.

Those who had much got still more: big landowners found themselves free from debts, houseowners had their mortgages redeemed, big capitalists could repay their loans with devalued money. Entrepreneurs were able to buy the commodity called labor with money of steadily decreasing value. For example during the inflation, Hugo Stinnes, an industrialist, acquired 1,664 formerly independent enterprises with 300,000 workers.

In November 1923 inflation came to a halt with an exchange rate of one U.S. dollar equal to 4.2 billion paper marks. One billion paper marks now equalled the newly created mark.

Militarism, or the acceptance of military ways of thinking and of military notions of order into non-military spheres, prevailed in Germany before and during World War I, but also in the Weimar Republic. Here it was backed not only by the Reichswehr (defensive

Stahlhelm Day: color detachments in Berlin, September 3, 1932

Crown Prince August Wilhelm of Prussia, in SA uniform, making a propoganda speech for Hitler, Berlin 1932

forces), but still more vigorously by the Right, wishing to restore the monarchy, and by their organizations, such as the Stahlhelm (Steel helmet).

Hindenburg's popularity was in no way diminished by the lost war. Many Germans regarded him as *Ersatz-Kaiser*, the man to replace the emperor. In 1925 Hindenburg, as candidate of a coalition of the parties of the Right, was elected President of the Reich; in 1932, as candidate of the poltical center and the moderate parties of the Left, he was re-elected.

Although the property of German princes was confiscated after the November revolution there were also compensation agreements providing for cash payments in addition to the granting of lands. On February 2, 1926 the Reichstag was considering a bill for the final settlement of the compensation question. The Left opposed this bill with a demand for disinheritance without compensation. The German League for Human Rights formed an anticompensation committee which was joined mainly by Communist organizations, but also by the SPD and the Reichswehr. However, the referendum of June 20, 1926, intended to bring about disinheritance, failed. As a result the Länder (provinces) arrived at settlements with the princely dynasties. The dynasty of Hohenzollern, for instance, received about 150,000 acres and 15 million marks.

Stahlhelm on parade, headed by Hohenzollern princes, around 1927

Harzburg Front, October 1931

On January 5, 1919 the "German Workers' Party" (DAP) was founded in Munich. As of March 1920 the party called itself "National Socialist German Workers' Party (NSDAP). In September 1919 Lance-Corporal Adolf Hitler, as representative of the Reichswehr, joined the party. With his mainly racist anti-Communism and his fanatical anti-Semitism he swiftly became the focal point of the party. From the start, large sections of the nobility and middle classes supported him, above all financially, because they looked to him for the pacification of the masses. After Hitler's failed putsch against the government in November 1923, the NSDAP (National Socialist German Workers' Party) was temporarily disbanded. On April 1, 1924 Hitler was sentenced to five years' detention in a fortress, but was granted an amnesty towards the end of 1924. While in prison at Landsberg on Lech he wrote the book *Mein Kampf*, which contained his political program. By 1933 about two million copies had been printed.

One of the most powerful men of the political Right in the Weimar Republic was the industrialist Alfred Hugenberg. From 1909 to 1918 he was chairman of the board of directors of Krupp, the munitions firm. Since 1916 he had been engaged in building up the Hugenberg group of companies, including the *Ufa* film company, the Scherl publishing house and the *Telegraphen-Union*. Through these undertakings the political Right—from 1928 Hugenberg was also party chairman of the "German-National People's Party" (DNVP)—gained enormous influence on public opinion.

On November 13, 1918 the factory owner Franz Seldte founded an association of front-line soldiers, called Der Stahlhelm (Steel helmet). By the mid-twenties the Stahlhelm had about 400,000 members. It fought against Marxism, against the peace treaty of Versailles, and against the parliamentary system. After the seizure of power by the National Socialists, the Stahlhelm placed itself under Hitler's leadership and was gradually absorbed into the "Storm Troopers" (SA), a military unit of the Nazis.

In 1931, under the leadership of Hugenberg, Hitler, Seldte and General von der Goltz, National Socialists, German-Nationals, Stahlhelm and other organizations were welded into the Harzburg front. At the Harzburg meeting of October 11, 1931 the Front declared itself ready to seize power.

Reichsjugend Day, 1934

The Harzburg Front collapsed in the spring of 1932, since a number of German-Nationals refused to support Hitler's election as President of the Reich.

In January 1933 the National Socialists seized power without putsch or public resistance. The civil parties as well as the Social Democrats and opposing Communists relinquished the Republic without a fight. During the last free elections in November 1932 the National Socialists had received only 33.5% of the votes. Nevertheless, Hitler was appointed Chancellor of the Reich by Hindenburg. This victory was largely due to the support given by the industrialists. Other contributing factors were the dissension among political parties, the inexperience of the masses with respect to the democratic process, and the widespread unemployment as a result of the international economic crisis. Immediately following Hitler's accession to power all fundamental democratic rights were abolished.

In November 1933, after the suppression of all other parties, the NSDAP (National Socialist German Workers' Party) captured 92% of the votes which came from all social classes of the German population.

The Berlin Years

1. *Nachtstück (Berlin-Südende)*, 1915.

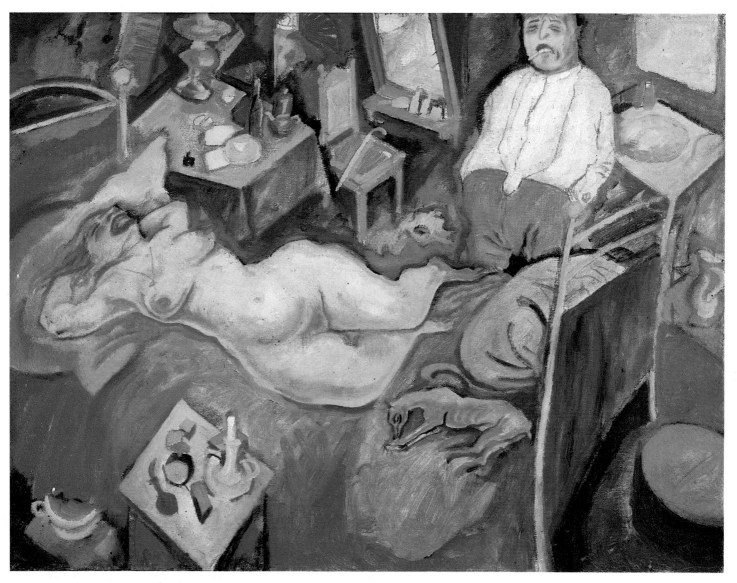

2. *Paar in Zimmer*, 1915.

3. *Die Strasse*, 1915.

4. *Explosion*, 1917.

5. *John, der Frauenmörder*, 1918.

6. *Seiltänzer*, 1918.

7. *Stützen der Gesellschaft*, 1926.

8. *Mann und Frau*, 1926.

9. *Sonnenfinsternis*, 1926.

10. *Lotte in grünem Kleid*, 1926.

11. *Eva Grosz*, 1927.

12. *Frau in schwarzem Mantel*, 1927.

13. *Landschaft Pointe Rouge (bei Marseille)*, 1927.

14. *Pointe Rouge (bei Marseille)*, 1927.

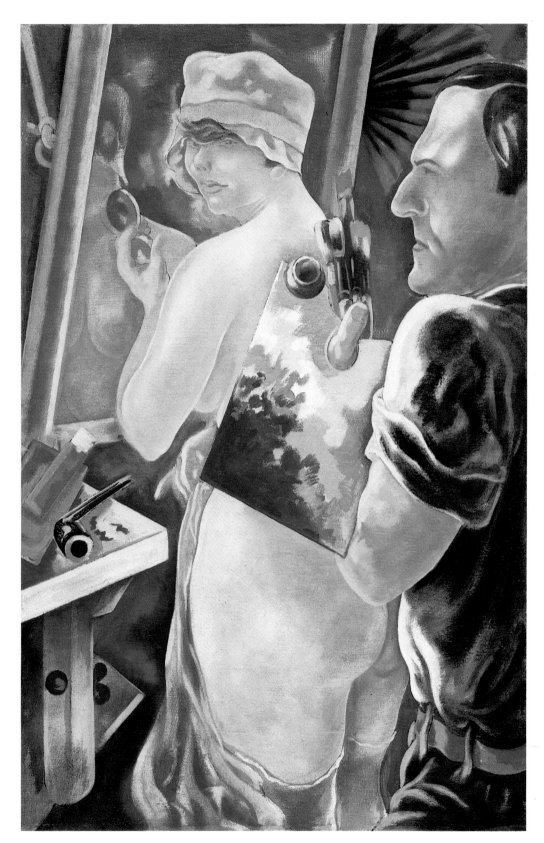

15. *Selbstportrait mit Modell,* 1928.

16. *Jahrmarkt*, 1928-29.

17. *Rudolf Schlichter*, 1929.

18. *Stilleben mit Katze und Augengläsern,* 1929.

19. *Zwei Akte*, 1929.

20. *Schlachter*, 1930.

21. *Akt mit schwarzen Strümpfen*, 1930.

22. *Stilleben mit Maske und Fisch*, 1931.

23. *Berliner Strasse*, 1931.

24. *Stilleben mit Handschuhen,*1931.

25. *Café "Verlorenes Glück"*, 1912.

26. *Selbstmörder*, 1912.

27. *Auf dem Weg zur Arbeit,* 1912.

28. *Buchumschlag zu Felix Holländer "Sturm im Westen"*, 1912.

29. *Buchumschlag zu Hermann Stehr "Leonore Griebel", 1912.*

30. *Strassenschlacht*, 1912.

31. *Streit in einer Kneipe*, 1912.

32. *Circe*, 1912-13.

33. *Wie ich mir Edgar Allan Poe vorstelle*, 1913.

34. *Lustmord*, 1913-14.

35. *Strassenszene*, 1915.

36. *Skizze zu Ölbild "Café"*, 1915.

37. *Cafészene*, 1915.

38. *Mann im Café*, 1915.

39. *Nachtcafé*, 1915.

40. *Lina Pantzer*, 1915.

41. *Akrobaten*, 1915.

42. *Stepptänzer*, 1915.

43. *Essender Mann*, 1916.

44. *Akte*, 1916.

45. *Litographien*, 1916.

46. *Sitzender Akt*, 1916.

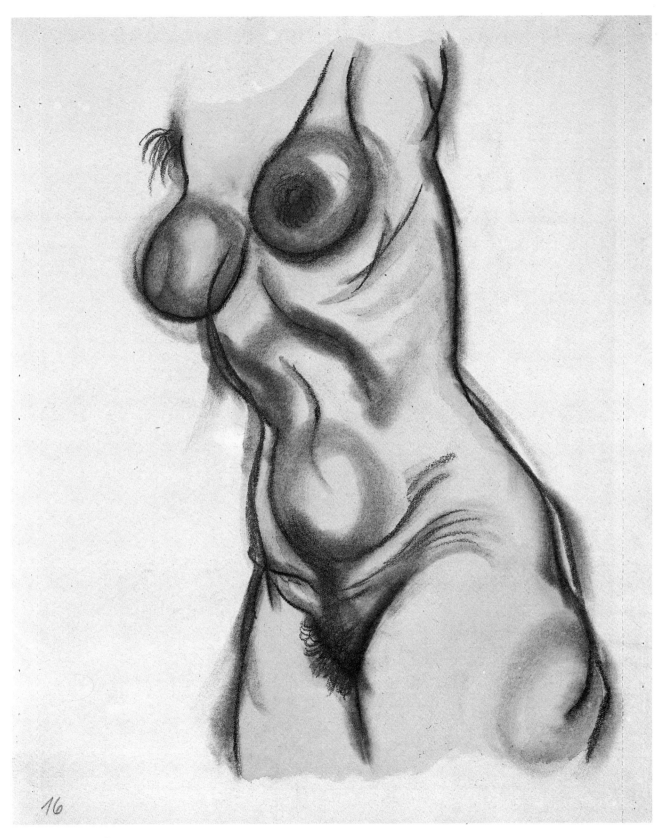

16

47. *Halbakt*, 1916.

48. *Zu Rachilde, "Der Liebesturm"*, 1916.

49. *In der Zelle*, 1917.

50. *Olympia-Kino, Berlin,* 1917.

51. *Unter der Laterne*, 1917.

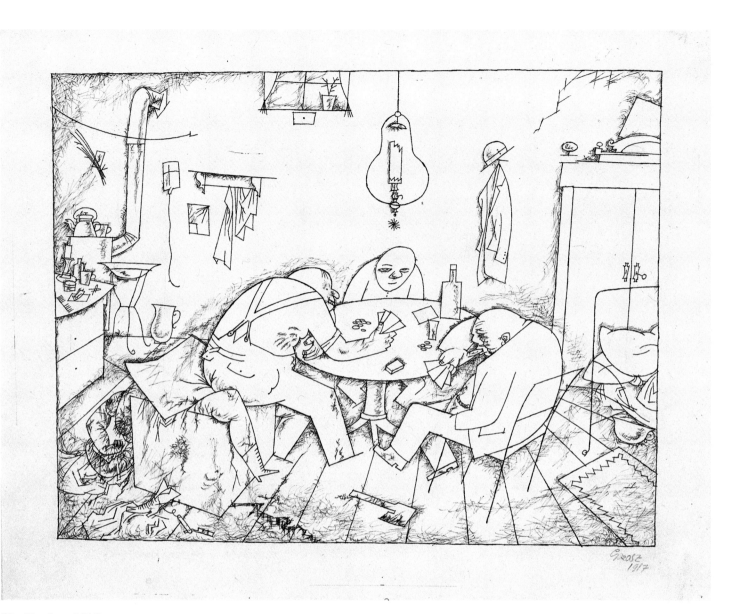

52. *Apachen*, 1917.

53. *Strassenszene*, 1917.

54. *Betrachtung*, 1917.

55. *Mann mit Messer, der eine Frau verfolgt,* 1917.

56. *Strassenszene*, 1917.

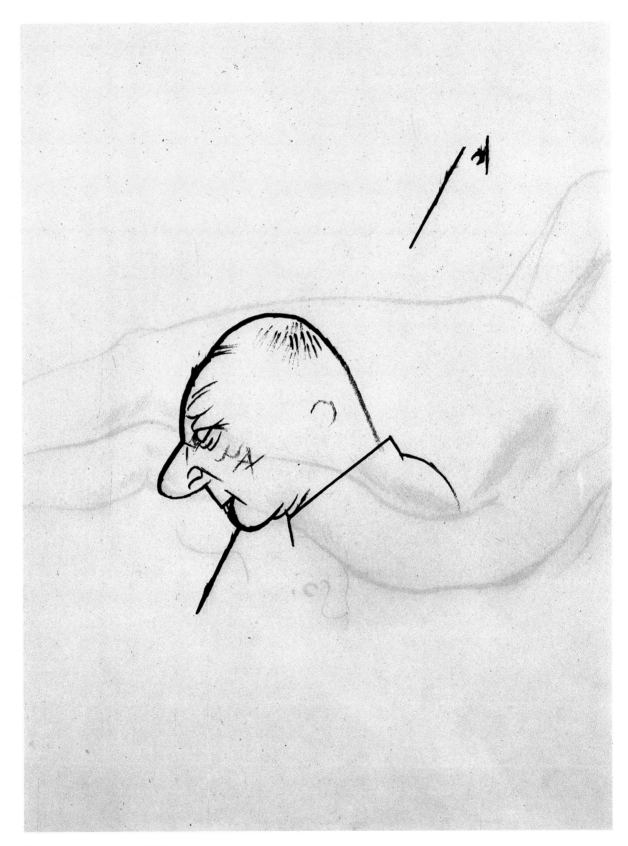

57. *Portraitstudie*, ca. 1918.

58. *Detektivgeschichte*, 1918.

59. *Chicago, A piece of my World*, 1918.

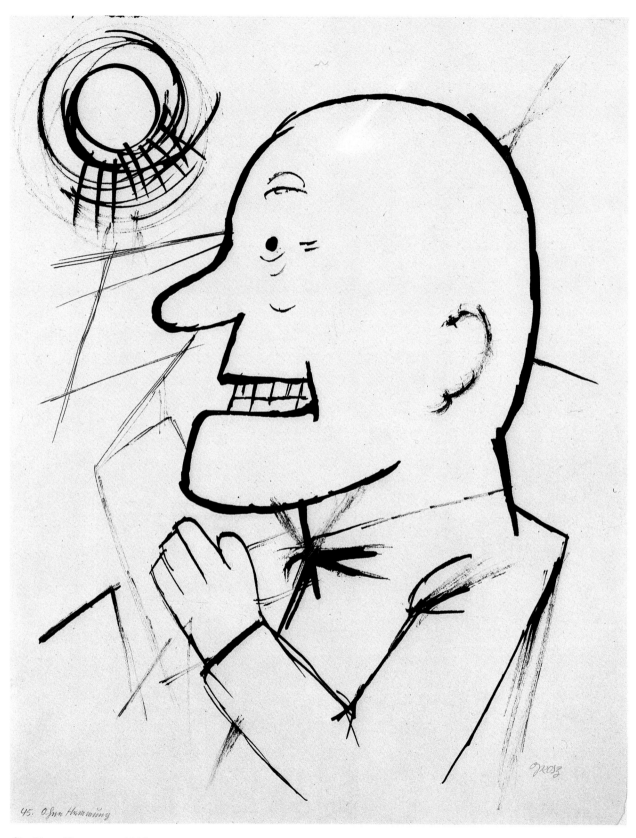

45. Ohne Hemmung

60. *Ohne Hemmung*, 1918.

61. *Selbstmörder*, 1918.

35

62. *Der absolute Monarchist*, 1918.

63. *Castors Panoptikum*, ca. 1918.

64. *Tragigrotesken des Wieland Herzfelde, 1919.*

65. *Café*, 1918-19.

66. *Paar*, 1919.

67. *Nieder mit Liebknecht*, 1919.

68. *Wiederaufbau*, 1919.

AGAMEMNON

69. *Agamemnon*, 1919.

70. *Wie der Staatsgerichtshof aussehen müsste!*, 1919.

71. *Schwere Zeiten*, 1919.

72. *Der blutige Ernst*, 1919.

73. *Hausherr*, 1919.

74. *Drei sitzende Leute im Profil*, 1919-20.

75. *Stehender Mann im Profil und Profil-Studie*, 1919-20.

76. *Stadtlandschaft*, 1920.

77. *Gruss aus Sachsen*, 1920.

78. *Gruss aus Sachsen*, 1920.

79. *Ku Klux Klan*, 1920.

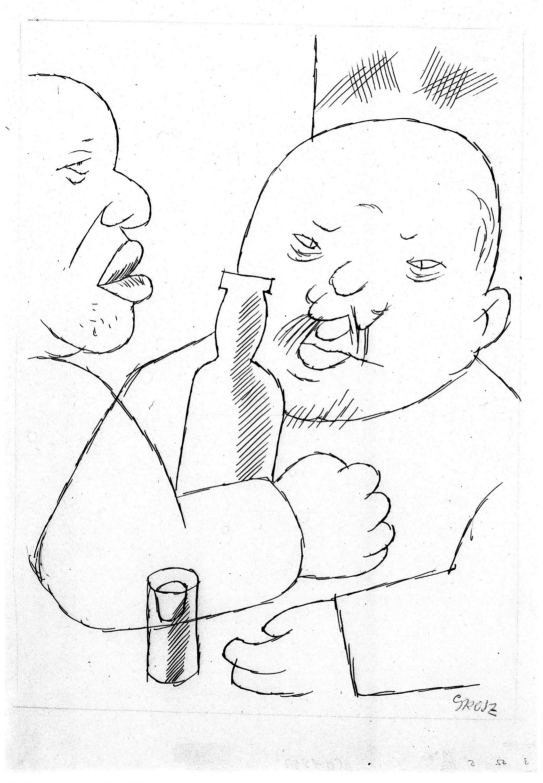

80. *Mann mit Flasche*, 1920.

81. *Bühnenbildentwurf zu G.B. Shaw, "Caesar und Cleopatra"*, 1920.

82. *Caesar*, 1920.

83. *Cleopatra,* 1920.

84. *Acht Figurinen zu "Caesar und Cleopatra", 1920.*

85. *Keep Smiling*, ca. 1920.

86. *Mann im Sessel,* ca. 1920.

87. *Zwei Männer*, ca. 1920.

88. *Leg all dein Leid auf Gott behertz/Vertrau dem Arzt/Auch wenn es schmerzt,* ca. 1920.

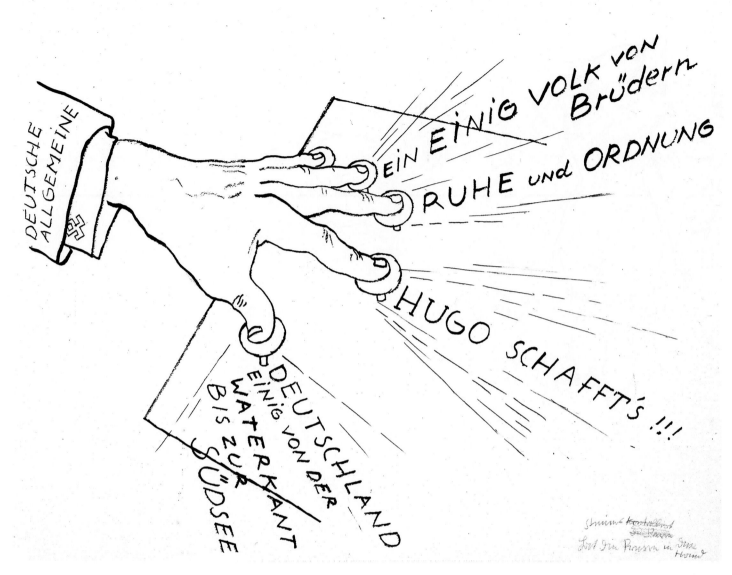

89. "*Deutsche Allgemeine*", 1920.

90. *Rede*, ca. 1920.

91. *Vertrautes Heim,* ca. 1920-21.

92. *Beim Frühstück*, 1921.

93. *Tartarins Traum,* 1921

94. *Schwimme, wer schwimmen kann, und wer zu plump ist, geh' unter!*, 1921.

95. *Im Wirtshaus*, 1921.

96. *Frau mit Laute*, 1921.

97. *Germanikus*, 1921.

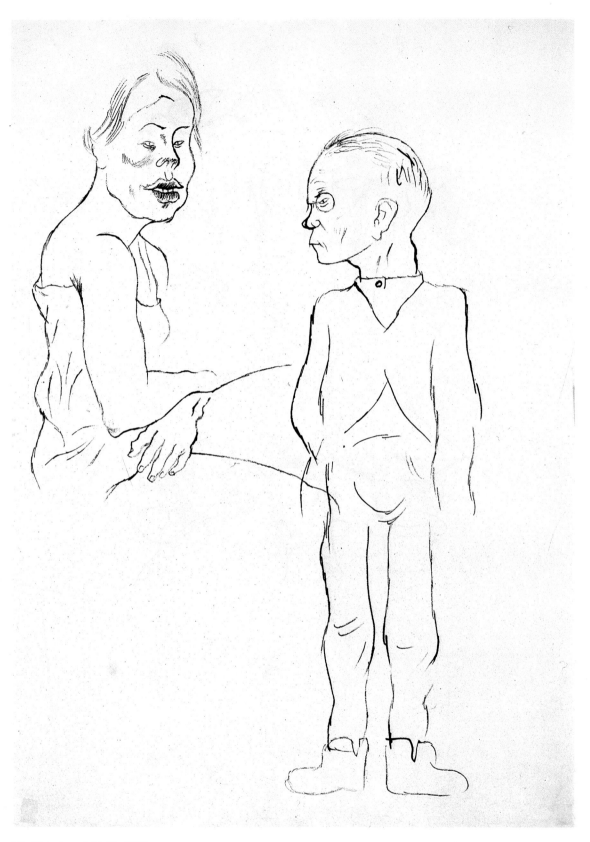

98. *Mann und Frau*, 1921.

99. *Germanentag*, 1921.

100. *Prost!*, 1921.

101. *Werbung,* 1921.

102. *Lady Hamiltons Schleiertanz*, 1921.

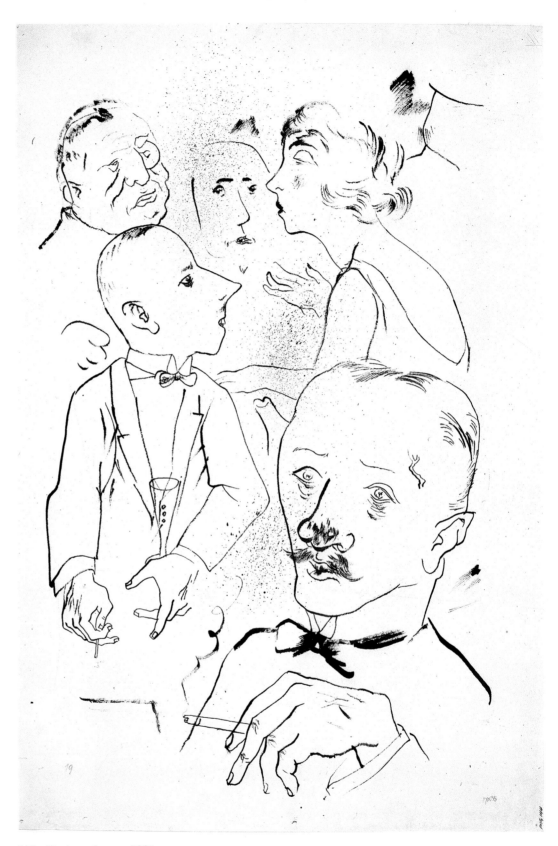

103. *Nachwuchs*, ca. 1921.

104. *Typenblatt*, ca. 1921.

105. *Blick in die Tauentzienstrasse* , ca. 1921.

106. *Hinrichtung*, 1922.

107. *Gottes sichtbarer Segen ist bei mir*, 1922.

108. *Der Dollar ist auf 300 Mark gestiegen*, 1922.

109. *Sonntag früh*, 1922.

110. *Ich will alles um mich her ausrotten, was mich einschränkt, dass ich nicht Herr bin*, 1922.

111. *Am Fenster*, ca. 1922.

Hoch Stinnes

112. *Hoch Stinnes*, ca. 1922.

113. *Streit (Grosz und Huelsenbeck)*, 1922.

114. *Die Schande*, 1922.

115. *Pappi und Mammi*, 1922.

116. *Drei Figurinen zu Georg Kaiser, ''Kanzlist Krehler'', 1922.*

117. *Das Paar*, 1922-24.

118. *Bund der Aufrechten*, 1922-24.

119. *Dolchstoss,* ca. 1922.

Schleusen Inspektor

120. *Schleuseninspektor*, 1923.

121. *Frau Schleuseninspektor*, 1923.

122. *Ebert (President Friedrich Ebert)*, ca. 1923.

Kuckuck

Papagei

Hirsch

Affe

Hund

Katze

123. *Tierkostümentwürfe,* 1922-23.

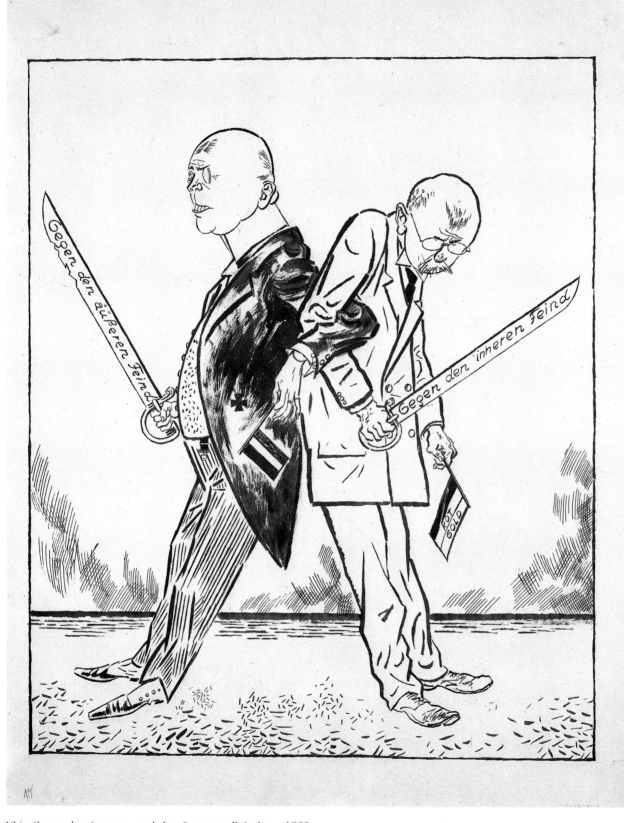

124. *Gegen den inneren und den äusseren Feind*, ca. 1923.

125. *Hunger,* ca. 1923.

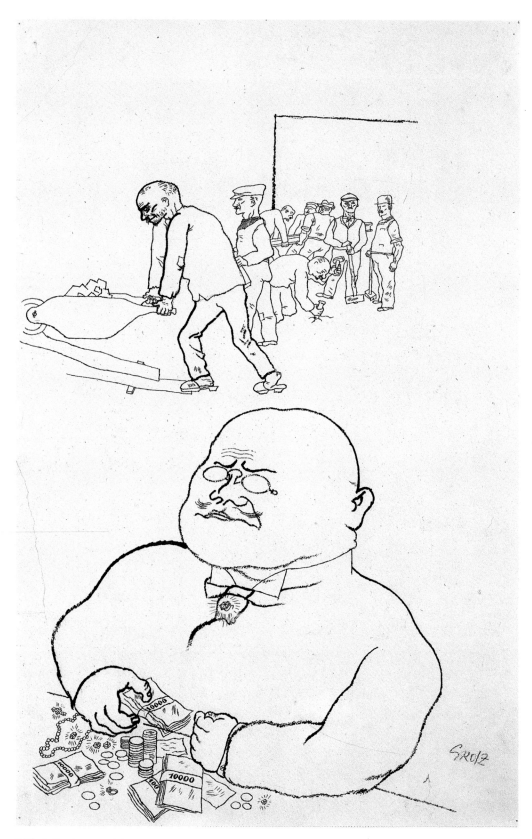

126. *Inflation*, ca. 1923.

127. *Paar und Tanzende*, ca. 1923.

128. *Garderobe in der Bar*, 1923.

129. *Figurine zu "Nebeneinander"*, 1923.

130. *Drei Beamte zu "Nebeneinander", 1923.*

131. *Figurine zu "Nebeneinander"*, 1923.

132. *Borsigs Schwester*, 1923.

133. *Pensionskorridor*, 1923.

134. *Nach dem Schiessen*, 1923.

145. *Megära*, 1924.

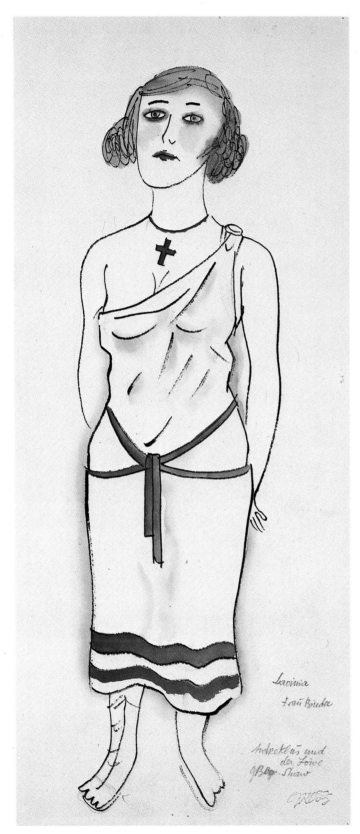

146. *Lavinia*, 1924.

147. *Hauptmann* 1924.

148. *Ida und ein Student*, 1924.

149. *Spaziergang*, 1924.

150. *Der Indifferente: ich wähle nicht*, ca. 1924.

151. *Wahl der KPD aus dem Gefängnis,* ca. 1924.

152. *Skat-Skizze*, ca. 1924.

155. *Der Sieg des republikanischen Gedankens,* 1925.

156. *Das Ende des Dr. Sand*, 1924-25.

159. *Hammer und Sichel,* ca. 1925.

160. *Oma Peter*, 1925.

161. *Schaufenster in Berlin*, 1926.

162. *Auf der Strasse,* ca. 1926.

163. *Hier sitz man gut*, 1927.

164. *Schwejk (Der Schauspieler Max Pallenberg)*, 1927.

165. *Der Militärarzt Dr. Bautze (Phase 6)*, 1927.

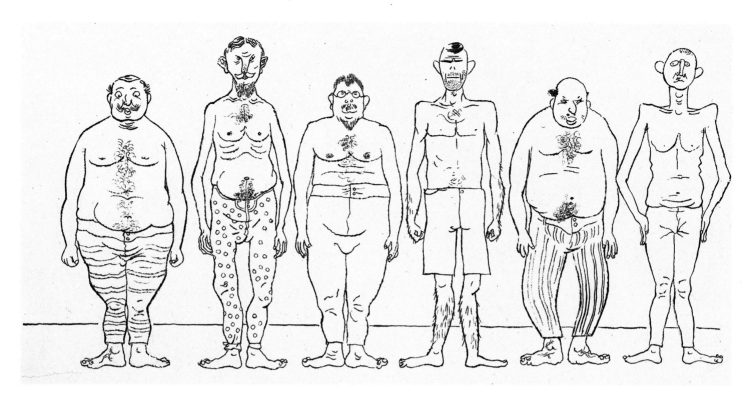

166. *Musterung*, 1927.

167. *Kein schöner Tod*, 1927.

168. *Die Obrigkeit*, 1927.

169. *Der Lebensbaum (Phase 2 und 3)*, 1927.

170. *Gewerkschaftssekretäre bei der Arbeit*, 1927.

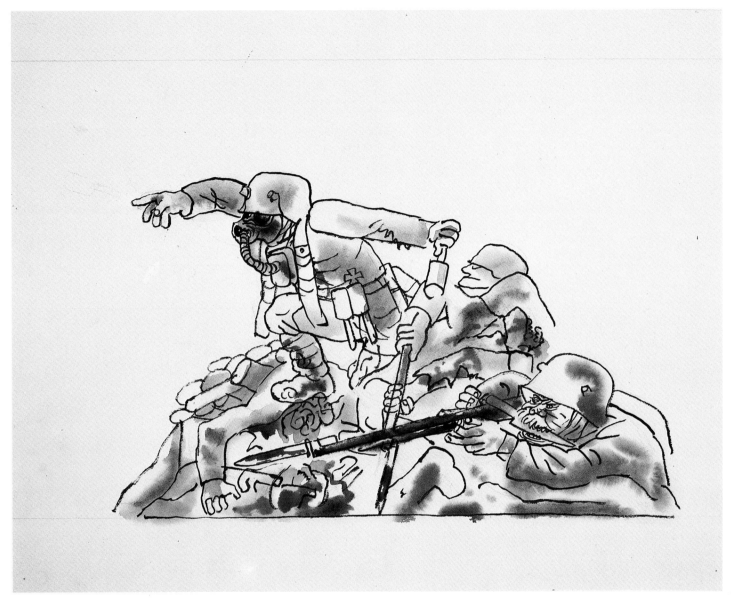

171. *Angriff*, 1927-28.

172. *Österreich wird ewig stehen!*, 1927-28.

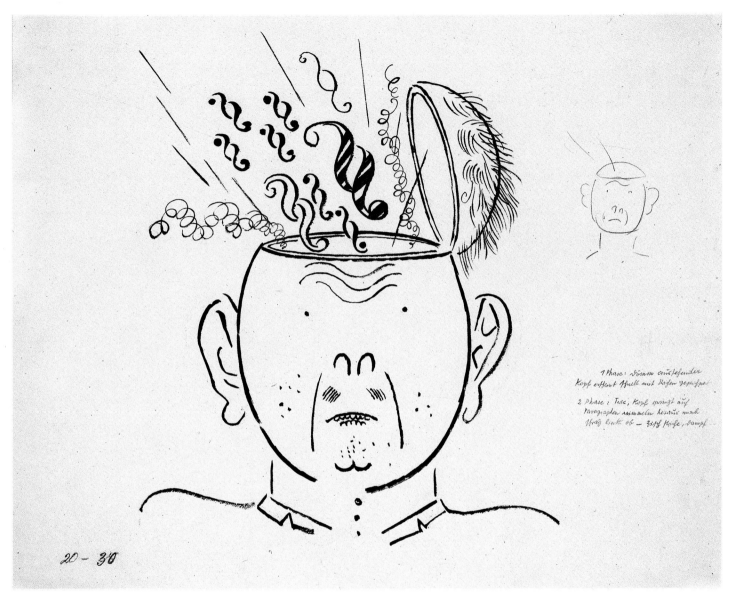

173. *Kopf mit geöffneter Schädeldecke*, 1927-28.

174. *Eleganter Herr mit Strohhut und Spazierstock*, 1927-28.

175. *Monteur*, 1927-28.

176. *Arbeiter mit Ballonmütze und Zeitung, 1927-28.*

177. *Offizier, 1927-28.*

Figurine zu Schwejk, Regie Piscator
fig. auf laufendem Band

178. *Figurine zu "Schwejk"*, 1927-28.

179. *Nachtwache*, 1927-28.

180. *Portraitstudie,* 1928.

181. *Strasse frei*, 1928.

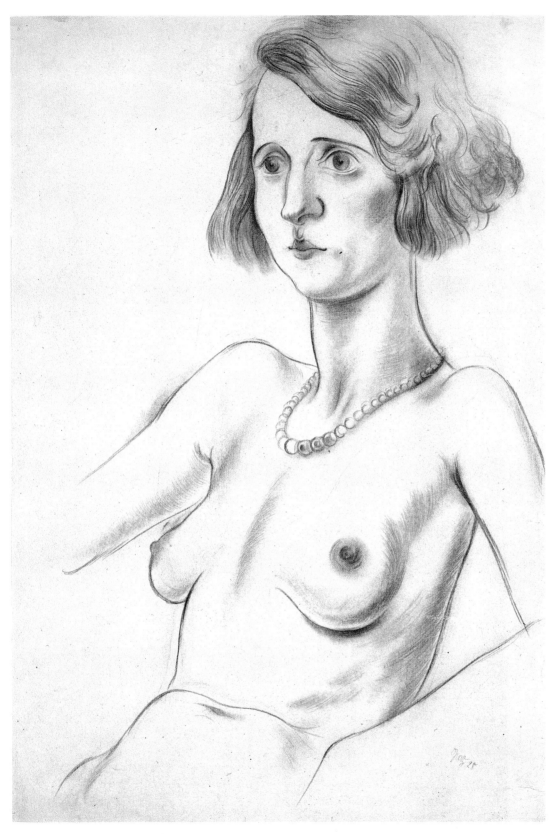

182. *Modell mit Halskette*, 1928.

183. *Akt mit blauem Halsband*, 1928.

184. *Emigranten*, 1928-30.

185. *Sitzender Akt*, 1929-30.

186. *Halbakt*, 1929.

187. *Akt mit blauen Schuhen*, 1929.

188. *Zwei Akte*, ca. 1929.

189. *Halbakt mit Schottenkostüm - Rückenansicht*, ca. 1929.

190. *Illustration zu "Die drei Soldaten" von Brecht*, 1930.

191. *Kartenspieler*, 1931.

LIST OF WORKS

1. "Nachtstück (Berlin-Südende)."
[Night-Piece ('Südende'—district in Berlin)], 1915.
Oil on canvas, 74.5 × 36.2 cm.
Signed and dated on verso.
Titled on verso: "Südende."
Nationalgalerie, Berlin.

2. "Paar im Zimmer."
(Couple in Interior), 1915.
Oil on canvas, 38.1 × 49.8 cm.
Signed and dated on verso.
Titled on verso: "Südende."

3. "Die Strasse."
(The Street), 1915.
Oil on canvas, 45.5 × 35.5 cm.
Staatsgalerie, Stuttgart.

4. "Explosion."
(Explosion), 1917.
Oil on board, 47.8 × 68.2 cm.
The Museum of Modern Art, New York.
Gift of Mr. and Mrs. Irwin Moskowitz.

5. "John, der Frauenmörder."
(John, the Sex Murderer), 1918.
Oil on canvas, 86.5 × 81 cm.
Hamburger Kunsthalle, Hamburg.

6. "Seiltänzer."
(Tightrope Walker), 1918.
Oil on canvas, 42 × 29 cm.

7. "Stützen der Gesellschaft."
(Pillars of Society), 1926.
Oil on canvas, 200 × 108 cm.
Signed and dated on verso.
Nationalgalerie, Berlin.

8. "Mann and Frau."
(Man and Woman), 1926.
Oil on canvas, 80 × 60 cm.

9. "Sonnenfinsternis."
(Eclipse of the Sun), 1926.
Oil on canvas, 218.4 × 188 cm.

Signed and dated on verso.
The Heckscher Museum,
Huntington, NY.

10. "Lotte in grünem Kleid."
(Lotte in Green Dress), 1926.
Oil on canvas, 93.3 × 72.4 cm.

11. "Eva Grosz," 1927.
Oil on canvas, 72.5 × 53.5 cm.
Signed and dated on verso.

12. "Frau in schwarzem Mantel."
(Standing Woman in Black Coat), 1927.
Oil on canvas, 128 × 83 cm.

13. "Landschaft Pointe Rouge (bei Marseille)."
[Landscape Pointe Rouge (near Marseille)], 1927.
Oil on canvas, 72.8 × 54.1 cm.
Signed, dated and titled on stretcher.

14. "Pointe Rouge (bei Marseille)."
[Pointe Rouge (near Marseille)], 1927.
Oil on board, 46.1 × 38 cm.

15. "Selbstportrait mit Modell."
(Artist and Model), 1928.
Oil on canvas, 115.6 × 75.6 cm.
The Museum of Modern Art, New York.
Gift of Mr. and Mrs. Leo Lionni, 1954.

16. "Jahrmarkt."
(Funfair), 1928–29.
Oil on canvas, 80.5 × 60 cm.

17. "Rudolf Schlichter," 1929.
Oil on canvas, 190 × 140 cm.
Signed and dated on verso.

18. "Stilleben mit Katze und Augengläsern."
(Still life with Cat and Eyeglasses), 1929.
Oil on canvas, 49 × 69 cm.
Signed and dated on verso.

19. "Zwei Akte."
(Two Nudes), 1929.
Oil on canvas, 220 × 115 cm.

20. "Schlachter."
(Butcher), 1930.
Oil on canvas, 81 × 66.5 cm.
Signed and dated lower left.

21. "Akt mit schwarzen Strümpfen."
(Nude with Black Stockings), 1930.
Oil on canvas, 72.4 × 58.4 cm.

22. "Stilleben mit Maske und Fisch."
(Still life with Mask and Fish), 1931.
Oil on canvas, 81 × 60 cm.

23. "Berliner Strasse."
(Berlin Street), 1931.
Oil on canvas, 81 × 60 cm.
Signed and dated lower left.
The Metropolitan Museum of Art,
New York.
Hugo Kastor Fund, 1963.

24. "Stilleben mit Handschuhen."
(Still life with Gloves), 1931.
Oil on canvas, 50 × 72 cm.
Signed and dated on verso.

25. "Café 'Verlorenes Glück.' "
(Café "Lost Fortune"), 1912.
Pen and ink and colored chalk,
22.9 × 21.3 cm.
Dated lower left.
Lilian and Peter Grosz, Princeton, NJ.

26. "Selbstmörder."
(Suicide), 1912.
Colored chalk, 22.8 × 28.8 cm.
Signed lower left.

27. "Auf dem Weg zur Arbeit."
(On the Way to Work), 1912.
Pen and ink, colored chalk and watercolor, 38.1 × 30.2 cm.
Lilian and Peter Grosz, Princeton, NJ.

28. "Buchumschlag zu Felix Holländer, *Sturm im Westen.*"
(Book-cover for *Sturm im Westen* by Felix Holländer), 1912.
Pen and ink and colored chalk, 18.5 × 13 cm.
Lilian and Peter Grosz, Princeton, NJ.

29. "Buchumschlag zu Hermann Stehr, *Leonore Griebel.*"
(Book-cover for *Leonore Griebel* by Hermann Stehr), 1912.
Pen and ink and watercolor, 29 × 23 cm.

30. "Strassenschlacht."
(Street Riot), 1912.
Brush and ink and black chalk, 25 × 37.7 cm.
Signed lower right.

31. "Streit in einer Kneipe."
(Bar Fight), 1912.
Crayon and watercolor, 22.2 × 27.7 cm.

32. "Circe," 1912/13.
Pen and ink, 21.2 × 33.2 cm.
Titled lower left.

33. "Wie ich mir Edgar Allan Poe vorstelle."
(Edgar Allan Poe), 1913.
Pen and ink and wash, 20.6 × 15.3 cm.
Signed lower right.
Titled lower left.

34. "Lustmord."
(Sex Murder), 1913/14.
Pen and ink, 16.6 × 24.1 cm.
Signed lower right.

35. "Strassenszene."
(Street Scene), 1915.
Black chalk, 33 × 21.1 cm.
Lilian and Peter Grosz, Princeton, NJ.

36. "Skizze zu Ölbild 'Kaffee.'"
(Sketch for the Painting "Café"), 1915.
Pen and ink, 32.8 × 21.2 cm.
Signed and dated lower right.
Titled lower left.

37. "Cafészene."
(Café Scene), 1915.
Pen and ink and colored chalk, 22.4 × 29.1 cm.
Signed lower right.
Dated lower left.
Lilian and Peter Grosz, Princeton, NJ.

38. "Mann im Café."
(Man in Café), 1915.
Black chalk, 32.9 × 21.1 cm.
Signed lower left.

39. "Nachtcafé."
(Café at Night), 1915.
Pen and ink and colored chalk, 28.4 × 22.5 cm.
Signed and titled lower right.

40. "Lina Pantzer," 1915.
Pencil, 29 × 22.5 cm.
Signed and titled lower right.
Reproduced in *Der Querschnitt*, March 1925.

41. "Akrobaten."
(Acrobats), 1915.
Pencil, 29 × 22.5 cm.

42. "Stepptänzer."
(Tap Dancers), 1915.
Pencil, 29.1 × 22.4 cm.
Signature stamp lower right.

43. "Essender Mann."
(Eating Man), 1916.
Brush and ink, 48.7 × 32.4 cm.
Signed lower right.

44. "Akte."
(Nudes), 1916.
Brush and ink, 47 × 31.7 cm.
Cover for the artist's portfolio of drawings.

45. "Lithografien."
(Lithographs), 1916.
Brush and ink, 62.7 × 43.2 cm.
Cover for the artist's portfolio of lithographs.

46. "Sitzender Akt."
(Seated Nude), 1916.
Pencil, 41 × 32.5 cm.
Signed lower right.

47. "Halbakt."
(Nude Torso), 1916.
Pencil and watercolor, 32.3 × 26.6 cm.
Dated lower left.
Lilian and Peter Grosz, Princeton, NJ.

48. "Zu Rachilde, *Der Liebesturm.*"
(Illustration to *Der Liebesturm* by Rachilde), ca. 1916.
Pencil, 29.8 × 22.5 cm.
Signed lower right.
Titled lower left.
Rachilde was the pseudonym for Marguerite Eymery, a writer of the 1880s famous for her novels that combine the horrible with the erotic.

49. "In der Zelle."
(Prison Cell), 1917.
Pen and ink, 51.5 × 36.5 cm.
Signed lower right.

50. "Olympia-Kino, Berlin."
("Olympia" Cinema in Berlin), 1917.
Pen and ink, 29 × 22.6 cm.
Lilian and Peter Grosz, Princeton, NJ.

51. "Unter der Laterne."
(Under the Lamppost), 1917.
Brush and ink and watercolor, 37.8 × 34.9 cm.
Signed lower right.

52. "Apachen."
(Apaches), 1917.
Pen and ink, 26.3 × 33.2 cm.
Signed and dated lower right.
Plate no. 58 in the portfolio "Ecce Homo," where it is dated 1916.
Dückers. S I, 58.

53. "Strassenszene."
(Street Scene), 1917.
Pen and ink, 28.5 × 22.5 cm.
Signed and dated lower right.

54. "Betrachtung."
(Inspection), 1917.
Pen and ink, 32.4 × 24.6 cm.
Signed lower right.
Lilian and Peter Grosz, Princeton, NJ.

55. "Mann mit Messer, der eine Frau verfolgt."
(Man with Knife Pursuing Woman), 1917.
Pen and ink and watercolor, 36.5 × 50.9 cm.

56. "Strassenszene."
(Street Scene), 1916.
Brush and ink, 31 × 20 cm.
Signed lower right.
Dated lower left.

57. "Portraitstudie."
(Male Portrait Study), ca. 1918.
Brush and ink, 38.5 × 51.7 cm.

58. "Detektivgeschichte."
(Detective Story), 1918.
Pen and ink, 58 × 46.5 cm.
Signed lower right.
Titled lower left.

59. "Chicago, A Piece of My World," 1918.
Pen and ink and watercolor, 47 × 53.3 cm.
Signed, dated and titled lower right.

60. "Ohne Hemmung."
(Without Inhibition), 1918.
Brush and ink, 34.9 × 27.7 cm.
Signed lower right.
Titled lower left.

61. "Selbstmörder."
(Suicide), 1918.
Pen and ink and watercolor, 50.8 × 36.5 cm.
Signed and dated lower right.

62. "Der absolute Monarchist."
(The Absolute Monarchist), 1918.
Brush and ink, 46 × 29.5 cm.
Signed lower right.
Plate no. 35 in the portfolio "Ecce Homo."
Dückers. S I, 35.

63. "Castors Panoptikum."
(Castor's Panopticum), ca. 1918.
Brush and ink and watercolor, 35 × 28 cm.
Signed lower left.
Bauhaus Archiv, Berlin.

64. "Tragigrotesken des Wieland Herzfelde."
(Tragigrotesques of Wieland Herzfelde), 1919.
Brush and ink, 49 × 30 cm.
Signed lower right.
Dückers. E 54.

65. "Café," 1918/19.
Pen and ink and watercolor, 24 × 31.8 cm.
Signed and dated lower left.

66. "Paar."
(Couple), 1919.
Pen and ink, 31 × 25.5 cm.
Signed lower right.

67. "Nieder mit Liebknecht."
(Down with Liebknecht), 1919.
Pen and ink and watercolor, 48.9 × 34.6 cm.
Signed lower right.

68. "Wiederaufbau."
(Reconstruction), 1919.
Pen and ink, 63 × 49.9 cm.

Variation of an illustration with the same title in the portfolio "Das Gesicht der herrschenden Klasse" (The Face of the Ruling Class).

69. "Agamemnon," 1919.
Pen and ink and watercolor, 48.8 × 37.4 cm.
Titled upper right.
Design for Walter Mehring's satirical marionette play Orestie, einfach klassisch (Oresteia—Simply Classical) in Berlin, 1919.

70. "Wie der Staatsgerichtshof aussehen müsste!"
(How the State Courts Ought to Look!), 1919.
Pen and ink, brush and ink, 54.2 × 37.5 cm.
Signed lower right.
Sketch for the title page of the satirical weekly Der blutige Ernst, special edition III: "Die Schuldigen."

71. "Schwere Zeiten."
(Hard Times), 1919.
Pen and ink, brush and ink, 39.7 × 30.3 cm.
Plate no. 27 in the portfolio "Ecce Homo."
Dückers. S I, 27.
Lilian and Peter Grosz, Princeton, NJ.

72. "Der blutige Ernst."
(The Bloody Truth), 1919.
Pen and ink, brush and ink, 56 × 59.5 cm.
Sketch for the satirical weekly Der blutige Ernst.

73. "Hausherr."
(Head of the Household), 1919.
Pen and ink, brush and ink, 47.5 × 30.5 cm.
Signed lower right.
Titled on verso.
Plate no. 29 in the portfolio "Ecce Homo," where it is dated 1919. Also reproduced in the portfolio "Die Gezeichneten" (The Designated). There it is dated 1921.
Dückers. S I, 29.

74. "Drei sitzende Leute im Profil."
(Three People Seated at Table), 1919/20.
Pen and ink, 36.8 × 29 cm.
Signed lower right.

75. "Stehender Mann im Profil und

Profil-Studie."
(Standing Man in Profile and Profile Study), 1919/20.
Pen and ink and black chalk, 50.3 × 33.7 cm.
Signed lower right.

76. "Stadtlandschaft."
(Cityscape), 1920.
Pen and ink, brush and ink, 52 × 41 cm.
Signed lower right.

77. "Gruss aus Sachsen."
(Greetings from Saxony), 1920.
Pen and ink and black chalk, 51.8 × 40.8 cm.
Titled and dated on verso.
Plate no. 5 in the portfolio "Ecce Homo."
Dückers. S I, 5.

78. "Gruss aus Sachsen."
(Greetings from Saxony), 1920.
Pen and ink, 58.8 × 42 cm.
Signed lower right.

79. "Ku Klux Klan," 1920.
Pen and ink, brush and ink, 65 × 52.2 cm.
Signed lower right.
Titled lower left.

80. "Mann mit Flasche."
(Man Hugging Bottle), 1920.
Pen and ink, 32.3 × 22.7 cm.
Signed lower right.

81. "Bühnenbildentwurf zu G.B. Shaw, Caesar und Cleopatra."
(Stage Design for Caesar and Cleopatra by G.B. Shaw), 1920.
Pen and ink and watercolor, 30.1 × 41.9 cm.
Titled and dated lower right.
Lilian and Peter Grosz, Princeton, NJ.

82. "Caesar," 1920.
Pencil and watercolor, 36 × 26.6 cm.
Titled lower right.

83. "Cleopatra," 1920.
Pen and ink and watercolor, 35.9 × 26.3 cm.
Titled lower right.

84. "Acht Figurinen zu G.B. Shaw, Caesar und Cleopatra."
(Eight Figurines for Caesar and Cleopatra by G.B. Shaw), 1920.
Pen and ink and watercolor, 45.5 × 40.8 cm.

Numbers 81, 82, 83 and 84 are stage and costume designs for G.B. Shaw's *Caesar and Cleopatra*, performed 1920 at the Deutsches Theater in Berlin.

85. "Keep Smiling," ca. 1920.
Brush and ink, 30.3 × 39.3 cm.
Titled lower left.
Sketch for Upton Sinclair's novel *100%*.

86. "Mann im Sessel."
(Seated Man), ca. 1920.
Pen and ink, 35.8 × 27.5 cm.

87. "Zwei Männer."
(Two Men), ca. 1920.
Pen and ink, 37.1 × 31 cm.
Signed lower right.

88. "Leg all dein Leid auf Gott beherzt/
Vertrau dem Arzt/Auch wenn es schmerzt."
(Bravely entrust your sorrow to God, but trust your doctor, even if it hurts), ca. 1920.
Pen and ink and pencil, 51 × 36.6 cm.
Titled lower right.

89. "Deutsche Allgemeine."
(German News), ca. 1920.
Brush and ink, 40.4 × 51.9 cm.

90. "Rede."
(Speech), ca. 1920.
Brush and ink, 55 × 37 cm.

91. "Vertrautes Heim."
(Domestic Bliss), ca. 1920/21.
Pen and ink, 44.1 × 33.9 cm.
Signed lower right.

92. "Beim Frühstück."
(Breakfast), 1921.
Pen and ink, 50.3 × 33.5 cm.
Signed lower right.

93. "Tartarins Traum."
(Tartarin's Dream), 1921.
Pen and ink, brush and ink, 49.8 × 32.6 cm.
Signed lower right.
Illustration for *The Adventures of the Tartarin from Tarascon* by Alphonse Daudet.
Dückers. BA I, 4.

94. "Schwimme, wer schwimmen kann, und wer zu plump ist, geh' unter!"
(Let those swim who can—the heavy may sink!), 1921.
Pen and ink, brush and ink,

52 × 40.5 cm.
Plate no. 8 in the portfolio "Die Räuber" (Nine lithographs to quotes from Schiller's play *The Robbers*). The title is from Act I, Scene I.
In addition the drawing is published in the portfolio "The Designated" with the title "Victory of the Machine"; in the journal *Der Gegner*, 1920/21, issue 8/9, entitled "…and allow the unemployed his daily money so he can die"; also in the third edition 1921 of "Das Gesicht"; and in the novel *Die rote Woche* (Berlin, 1921) by Franz Jung with the title "It is the proletariat's disease to be a human being who is striving towards the light but is always pushed back into hopelessness."
Dückers. M V, 8.

95. "Im Wirtshaus."
(At the Tavern), 1921.
Pen and ink, 65 × 52.2 cm.
Signed lower right.

96. "Frau mit Laute."
(Woman with Lyre), 1921.
Pen and ink, 51.7 × 35.2 cm.
Signed lower right.

97. "Germanikus."
(Germanicus), 1921.
Pen and ink, brush and ink, 64.7 × 48.7 cm.
Signed lower right.
Titled lower left.

98. "Mann und Frau."
(Man and Woman), 1921.
Pen and ink, brush and ink, 58.7 × 39.9 cm.

99. "Germanentag."
(Teutonic Celebration), 1921.
Pen and ink, 45.8 × 37 cm.
Plate no. 43 in the portfolio "Ecce Homo."
Also reproduced in the journal *Der Knüppel*, No. 5, August 10, 1924.
Dückers. S I, 43.

100. "Prost!"
(Cheers!), 1921.
Pen and ink and black chalk, 49.9 × 32.2 cm.
Signed lower right.

101. "Werbung."
(Solicitation), 1921.
Pen and ink, 39.2 × 29.5 cm.

Variation of the illustration "Für Regentage" (For Rainy Days) for the book *Munkepunke Dionysos* by Alfred Richard Meyer.
Dückers. B I, 3.

102. "Lady Hamiltons Schleiertanz."
(Lady Hamilton's Veil Dance), 1921.
Brush and ink, 57.7 × 45.2 cm.
Signed lower right.
Variation of an illustration for the book *Lady Hamilton* by Alfred Richard Meyer.
Dückers. B II, 4.

103. "Nachwuchs."
(The New Generation), ca. 1921.
Pen and ink, brush and ink and splatter, 58.9 × 39.7 cm.
Signed lower right.
Plate no. 19 in the portfolio "Ecce Homo."
Dückers S I, 19.
Lilian and Peter Grosz, Princeton, NJ.

104. "Typenblatt."
(Sketches of Prototypes), ca. 1921.
Pen and ink, brush and ink, 43.2 × 55.5 cm.
Signed lower right.
Titled lower left.

105. "Blick in die Tauentzienstrasse."
(View of the 'Tauentzienstrasse'), ca. 1921.
Pen and ink and black chalk, 53.3 × 43.8 cm.
Signed lower right.
Titled lower left.

106. "Hinrichtung."
(Execution), 1922.
Pen and ink, 54.6 × 40.3 cm.
Signed and dated lower right.
Variation of plate no. 84 in the portfolio "Ecce Homo."
Dückers. S I, 84.

107. "Gottes sichtbarer Segen ist bei mir."
(The blessing of heaven is visibly upon me), 1922.
Pen and ink, brush and ink and splatter, 56.5 × 46 cm.
Titled lower right.
Plate no. 6 in the portfolio "Die Räuber" (Nine lithographs to quotes from Schiller's play *The Robbers*). The title is from Act II, Scene 3.

In addition the drawing is published in the portfolio "The Designated" with the title "The blessing of heaven is visible upon us" (Schiller). It also appears in the portfolio "The Reckoning Follows!" as "A beloved wife and a lovable child are my heaven on earth."
Dückers. M V, 6.

108. "Der Dollar ist auf 300 Mark gestiegen."
(The Dollar Advanced to 300 Marks), 1922.
Pen and ink, 56 × 46 cm.
Signed lower right.
Titled lower left.
Plate in the portfolio "Abrechnung folgt!" (The Reckoning Follows!).

109. "Sonntag früh."
(Sunday Morning), 1922.
Brush and ink, 63 × 50.1 cm.
Signed lower right.
Titled lower left.
Plate no. 78 in the portfolio "Ecce Homo."
Dückers. S I, 78.

110. "Ich will alles um mich her ausrotten, was mich einschränkt, dass ich nicht Herr bin."
(I will root up from my path whatever obstructs my progress toward becoming the master), 1922.
Pen and ink, brush and ink and splatter, 63 × 50 cm.
Plate no. 1 in the portfolio "Die Räuber" (Nine lithographs to quotes from Schiller's play *The Robbers*). The title is from Act I, Scene 1.
In addition the drawing is published in the portfolio "The Designated" with the title "Of One's Own Strength" and in the portfolio "The Reckoning Follows!" as "The Director."
Dückers. M V, 1.

111. "Am Fenster."
(At the Window), ca. 1922.
Pen and ink, 55 × 39 cm.

112. "Hoch Stinnes."
(Cheers Stinnes *), ca. 1922.
Pen and ink, 33.5 × 31 cm.
Signed on verso.

113. "Streit" (Grosz und Huelsenbeck).
(Dispute between Grosz and the Author Huelsenbeck), 1922.
Brush and ink and watercolor, 50 × 39.2 cm.

114. "Die Schande."
(The Disgrace), 1922.
Pen and ink, brush and ink and watercolor, 63 × 50 cm.
Sketch for a book cover.

115. "Pappi und Mammi."
(Daddy and Mommy), 1922.
Pen and ink and watercolor, 47.8 × 41.4 cm.
Signed lower right.
Titled lower right on verso.

116. "Drei Figurinen zu Georg Kaiser, *Kanzlist Krehler.*"
(Three Figurines for *Kanzlist Krehler* by George Kaiser), 1922.
Pen and ink and watercolor, 45.9 × 56.5 cm.

117. "Das Paar."
(The Couple), ca. 1922/24.
Pen and ink and watercolor, 57.5 × 40 cm.
Signed lower right.

118. "Bund der Aufrechten."
(Pillars of Society), ca. 1922/23.
Pen and ink, brush and ink, 66 × 41.5 cm.
Titled upper center.

119. "Dolchstoss."
(Stab in the Back), ca. 1922.
Brush and ink, 59.4 × 46 cm.
Signed lower right.
Variation of an illustration with the same title in the portfolio "Die Gezeichneten" (The Designated).

120. "Schleuseninspektor."
(Lock-Inspector), 1923.
Brush and ink and watercolor, 50 × 39.3 cm.
Titled lower right.

121. "Frau Schleuseninspektor."
(Wife of Lock-Inspector), 1923.
Brush and ink and watercolor, 50 × 39.3 cm.

Titled lower right.

122. "Ebert."
(President Friedrich Ebert), ca. 1923.
Pen and ink, brush and ink, 40 × 29.3 cm.
Signed lower right.

123. "Tierkostümentwürfe."
(Animal Costume Designs), 1922/23.
Pen and ink and watercolor, 41.2 × 52.5 cm.

124. "Gegen den inneren und den äusseren Feind."
(Against the Inner and Outer Enemy), ca. 1923.
Pen and ink, brush and ink, 64.9 × 52.4 cm.

125. "Hunger."
(Hunger), ca. 1923.
Brush and ink, 49.9 × 39.3 cm.
Sketch for plate no. 57 in the portfolio "Der Spiesser-Spiegel" (Mirror of the Philistine).

126. "Inflation."
(Inflation), ca. 1923.
Pen and ink, brush and ink and black chalk, 50 × 32.5 cm.
Signed lower right.
Lilian and Peter Grosz, Princeton, NJ.

127. "Paar und Tanzende."
(Couple and Dancers), ca. 1923.
Brush and ink and watercolor, 58.3 × 40 cm.
Similar to plate no. 36 in the portfolio "Der Spiesser-Spiegel" (Mirror of the Philistine).

128. "Garderobe in der Bar."
(Checkroom of a Bar), 1923.
Pen and ink and watercolor, 36.3 × 49.7 cm.

129. "Figurine zu *Nebeneinander.*"
(Figurine for *Nebeneinander*), 1923.
Brush and ink and watercolor, 48.5 × 28 cm.
Titled lower right.

130. "Drei Beamte zu *Nebeneinander.*"
(Three Civil Servants for *Nebeneinander*), 1923.
Pen and ink and watercolor, 39.3 × 50 cm.

* For reference to the industrialist Hugo Stinnes, see article by Marina Schneede-Sczesny.

131. "Figurine zu *Nebeneinander*."
(Figurine for *Nebeneinander*), 1923.
Pen and ink and watercolor,
49.9 × 23.9 cm.
Titled lower right.

132. "Borsigs Schwester."
(Borsig's Sister), 1923.
Brush and ink and watercolor,
46.1 × 31.2 cm.
Titled lower right.

133. "Pensionskorridor."
(Rooming House Hallway), 1923.
Watercolor and pencil, 36.2 × 49.8 cm.
Signed lower right.
Titled lower left.

Numbers 120, 121 and 128–133 are stage
and costume designs for Georg Kaiser's
play *Nebeneinander*, performed in 1923 at
the Lustspielhaus, Berlin.

134. "Nach dem Schiessen."
(After the Shooting), 1923.
Pen and ink, brush and ink, 50 × 60 cm.
Signed lower right.

135. "Sie macht nur sauber."
(She Only Cleans), 1924.
Pencil, 59.1 × 47.5 cm.
Signed and titled lower right.
Plate no. 19 in the portfolio "Das neue
Gesicht der herrschenden Klasse" (The
New Face of the Ruling Class).

136. "Kabarett."
(Cabaret), 1924.
Brush and ink and splatter,
58.6 × 40.2 cm.

137. "Arbeitsloser."
(Unemployed Man), 1924.
Pencil, 63 × 50.4 cm.

138. "Die Zuchthaus-Republik."
(The Prison-Republic), 1924.
Brush and ink, 62.9 × 50 cm.

139. "Strasse frei."
(Make Way!), 1924.
Pen and ink, brush and ink,
65 × 52.3 cm.
Signed and dated lower left.
The drawing was originally intended as
illustration for *Strasse frei*, a collection of
poems by Oskar Kanehl. With the title
"Sheet-Lightning" it is plate no. 60 in the
portfolio "Das Neue Gesicht der
herrschenden Klasse" (The New Face of

the Ruling Class).

140. "Stehender Akt."
(Standing Nude), 1924.
Pencil, 63 × 50 cm.

141. "Akt mit verschränkten Armen."
(Nude with Folded Arms), 1924.
Pencil, 60 × 46.4 cm.

142. "Drei Figuren."
(Three Figures), ca. 1924.
Pen and ink, brush and ink,
34 × 35.2 cm.
Signed lower right.

143. "Ein Wanderliedchen."
(Hiking Song), ca. 1924.
Pen and ink, 63 × 48 cm.
Signature stamp lower right.
Titled lower left.
With the title "Jumheidi! Jumheida!"
plate no. 11 in the portfolio "Das neue
Gesicht der herrschenden Klasse" (The
New Face of the Ruling Class).

144. "Paar im Profil."
(Couple in Profile), ca. 1924.
Pen and ink, 40.5 × 34.6 cm.
Signed lower right.

145. "Megaera," 1924.
Brush and ink and watercolor,
50 × 39.3 cm.
Titled lower right.

146. "Lavinia," 1924.
Brush and ink and watercolor,
47.7 × 20.8 cm.
Signature stamp lower right.
Titled lower right.

Numbers 145 and 146 are costume
designs for George Bernhard Shaw's
Androkles und der Löwe (*Androcles and the
Lion*), performed in 1924 at the Residenz
Theater, Berlin.

147. "Hauptmann."
(Captain), 1924.
Pen and ink and watercolor, 48 × 23 cm.
Titled lower right.

148. "Ida und ein Student."
(Ida and the Student), 1924.
Watercolor, 41.1 × 53 cm.
Titled to the right of each figure.
Costume designs for Iwan Goll's
Methusalem oder der Ewige Bürger
(*Methusalem: The Eternal Bourgeois*) which

were not used in the first production
(1924) at the Dramatische Theater in
Berlin.

149. "Spaziergang."
(Promenade), 1924.
Pen and ink and watercolor,
75.6 × 57.2 cm.
Signed lower left.

150. "Der Indifferente: ich wähle nicht."
(The Indifferent Man: I Don't Vote),
ca. 1924.
Pen and ink, brush and ink,
64.9 × 52.4 cm.
Titled upper right.
Variation of plate no. 29 titled "Ich will
von Politik nichts wissen" (I am not
interested in politics) in the portfolio "Das
neue Gesicht der herrschenden Klasse"
(The New Face of the Ruling Class).

151. "Wahl der KPD aus dem
Gefängnis."
(Casting a Vote from Prison for the
German Communist Party), ca. 1924.
Brush and ink, 65 × 52.3 cm.

152. "Skat-Skizze."
(Sketch of Card Players), ca. 1924.
Brush and ink, 59 × 46 cm.
Signed lower right.
Titled lower left.

153. "Plauderei."
(Chat), 1925.
Pen and ink and watercolor,
75.3 × 56.8 cm.
Signed and dated lower right.

154. "Neunzehnhundertsiebzehn."
(Nineteen Hundred and Seventeen),
ca. 1925.
Brush and ink, 64.8 × 52.3 cm.
Signature stamp lower right.

155. "Der Sieg des republikanischen
Gedankens."
(The Victory of the Republican Idea),
1925.
Brush and ink and watercolor,
50.1 × 68 cm.

156. "Das Ende des Dr. Sand."
(Dr. Sand's End), 1924/25.
Pen and ink, 64.8 × 52.3 cm.
Signed lower left.
Titled on verso.
Variation of the illustration with the same
title for Heinrich Mann's short story

Kobes. With the title "Schwarzer Freitag" (Black Friday) it is plate no. 22 in the portfolio "Das neue Gesicht der herrschenden Klasse" (The New Face of the Ruling Class).
Dückers. B III, 10.

157. "Matrose im Nachtlokal."
(Sailor in Nightclub), 1925.
Watercolor, 70 × 50.2 cm.
Signed and dated lower left.

158. "Verehrung."
(Reverence), ca. 1925.
Pencil, 59.4 × 45.9 cm.
Signed lower right.

159. "Hammer und Sichel."
(Hammer and Sickle), ca. 1925.
Brush and ink, 65 × 52.6 cm.

160. "Oma Peter."
(Grandmother Peter), 1925.
Pencil, 60.1 × 46.4 cm.

161. "Schaufenster in Berlin."
(Shop Windows in Berlin), 1926.
Pen and ink, brush and ink,
62.5 × 45 cm.
Signed and dated lower right.
Lilian and Peter Grosz, Princeton, NJ.

162. "Auf der Strasse."
(Street Scene), ca. 1926.
Pen and ink and watercolor,
50.8 × 69.9 cm.
Signed and titled lower right.
Lilian and Peter Grosz, Princeton, NJ.

163. "Hier sitzt man gut."
(Café Scene), 1927.
Brush and ink, 47.4 × 62.9 cm.
Signed and dated lower right.
Titled lower left.
Plate no. 68 in the portfolio "Über alles die Liebe" (Love Above All).
Lilian and Peter Grosz, Princeton, NJ.

164. "Schwejk."
(Schwejk—The Actor Max Pallenberg), 1927.
Brush and ink, 59.4 × 46 cm.
Titled lower right.
With the title "Schwejk: 'melde gehorsamst, dass ich blöd' bin' " (Beg to report, Sir, I am an idiot) plate no. 1 in the portfolio "Hintergrund" (Background).
Dückers. M VI, 1.

165. "Der Militärarzt Dr. Bautze (Phase 6)."
(Dr. Bautze, Phase 6), 1927.
Pen and ink, brush and ink and splatter, 48.6 × 63 cm.
Signed lower right.
Titled on verso.
With the title "Ich liebe Dich!" (I love you) plate no. 5 in the portfolio "Hintergrund" (Background).
Dückers. M VI, 5.

166. "Musterung."
(Inspection), 1927.
Brush and ink, 52.1 × 65 cm.
Titled on verso.
With the title "Das ganze Volk ist eine Simultanenbande" (The Entire Population is a Bunch of Malingerers) plate no. 6 in the portfolio "Hintergrund" (Background).
Dückers. M VI, 6.

167. "Kein schöner Tod."
(Not a Nice Way of Dying), 1927.
Black chalk, 21.5 × 14 cm.
Signed and dated lower right.
Plate no. 76 in the portfolio "Die Gezeichneten" (The Designated).
With the title "Mir ist der Krieg wie eine Badekur bekommen" (The War Did Me a Lot of Good, Like a Spa) plate no. 12 in the portfolio "Hintergrund" (Background).
Dückers. M VI, 12.

168. "Die Obrigkeit."
(The Authorities), 1927.
Brush and ink, 52.3 × 64.9 cm.
Signed and titled lower right.
With the title "Seid untertan der Obrigkeit" (Bow to the Authorities) plate no. 2 in the portfolio "Hintergrund" (Background).
Dückers. M VI, 2.

169. "Der Lebensbaum (Phase 2 und 3)."
(Tree of Life, Phase 2 and 3), 1927.
Brush and ink, 52 × 65 cm.
Plate no. 4 in the portfolio "Hintergrund" (Background).
Dückers. M VI, 4.

170. "Gewerkschaftssekretäre bei der Arbeit."
(The Racket), 1927.
Pen and ink, brush and ink and splatter, 68.2 × 42.9 cm.

Titled lower right.
Lilian and Peter Grosz, Princeton, NJ.

171. "Angriff."
(Attack), 1927/28.
Brush and ink and watercolor,
39.2 × 50 cm.

172. "Österreich wird ewig stehen!"
(Austria Will Stand Forever!), 1927/28.
Brush and ink, 52 × 65 cm.

173. "Kopf mit geöffneter Schädeldecke."
(Open Head With Paragraphs), 1927/28.
Brush and ink, 39.4 × 50.1 cm.

174. "Eleganter Herr mit Strohhut und Spazierstock."
(Gentleman with Straw Hat and Cane), 1927/28.
Pen and ink and watercolor,
50 × 39.4 cm.
Signed and titled lower right.

175. "Monteur."
(Mechanic), 1927/28.
Brush and ink and watercolor,
50 × 37 cm.
Signed lower center.
Titled on verso.

176. "Arbeiter mit Ballonmütze und Zeitung."
(Worker with Cap and Newspaper), 1927/28.
Pen and ink and watercolor,
50 × 39.4 cm.
Signed lower center.
Titled lower right.

177. "Offizier."
(Officer), 1927/28.
Pen and ink and watercolor,
50 × 39.3 cm.
Signed lower right.
Titled on verso.

178. "Figurine zu *Schwejk*."
(Figurine for *Schwejk*), 1927/28.
Pen and ink and watercolor,
50 × 39.2 cm.

179. "Nachtwache."
(Night Watch), 1927/28.
Brush and ink and splatter,
52.2 × 65 cm.

Numbers 164, 165, 166, 168, 169, and 171–179 are stage and costume designs for Erwin Piscator's staging in 1928 of *Die*

Abenteuer des braven Soldaten Schwejk (The Adventures of the Good Soldier Schwejk) by Jaroslav Hašek. Of the more than three hundred drawings which Grosz completed for the play, seventeen were selected for the portfolio "Hintergrund" (Background).

180. "Portraitstudie."
(Portrait Study), 1928.
Pencil, 59.3 × 44.4 cm.
Signed and dated lower right.

181. "Strasse frei."
(Make Way!), 1928.
Black chalk, 60.1 × 46.1 cm.
Signed and dated lower right.
Sketch for book cover for *Strasse frei* (*Make Way!*), a collection of poems by Oskar Kanehl.

182. "Modell mit Halskette."
(Model with Necklace), 1928.
Pencil, 72 × 49.5 cm.
Signed and dated lower right.
Titled on verso.

183. "Akt mit blauem Halsband."
(Nude with Blue Ribbon), 1928.
Pen and ink and watercolor,
72.6 × 51 cm.
Signed lower right.

184. "Emigranten."
(Emigrants), 1928/30.
Pen and ink, brush and ink, 66 × 46 cm.
Signature stamp lower right.

185. "Sitzender Akt."
(Seated Nude), 1929/30.
Watercolor, 66.2 × 48.7 cm.

186. "Halbakt."
(Semi-Nude), 1929.
Pen and ink and watercolor,
61.8 × 49.6 cm.

187. "Akt mit blauen Schuhen."
(Nude with Blue Shoes), 1929.
Pen and ink and watercolor,
65.8 × 47.5 cm.
Signed and dated lower right.

188. "Zwei Akte."

(Two Nudes), ca. 1929.
Pen and ink and watercolor,
67 × 47.8 cm.
Signed lower right.

189. "Halbakt mit Schottenkostüm—Rückenansicht."
(Semi-Nude in Scottish Attire—Back View), ca. 1929.
Pen and ink and watercolor,
64.9 × 33.1 cm.
Signed lower right.

190. "Illustration zu *Die drei Soldaten* von Brecht."
(Illustration for *The Three Soldiers* by Brecht), 1930.
Brush and ink, 60 × 44 cm.

191. "Kartenspieler."
(Card Players), 1931.
Pen and ink, brush and ink,
65.5 × 46.2 cm.
Illustration for "Amerika, Du hast es auch nicht besser" by Eddie Cantor in *Uhu*, Berlin, January 1932, issue 4, p. 57.

PORTFOLIOS, BOOKS OF DRAWINGS AND TEXTS BY GEORGE GROSZ

Erste George Grosz-Mappe. 9 original lithographs. Berlin: Heinz Barger Verlag, 1917.

Kleine Grosz-Mappe. 20 original lithographs. Berlin: Malik-Verlag, 1917.

Gott mit uns. 9 political lithographs. Berlin: Malik-Verlag, 1920.

Das Gesicht der herrschenden Klasse. 55 political drawings. Berlin: Malik-Verlag, 1921 (Kleine revolutionäre Bibliothek, 4).

Im Schatten. 9 lithographs. Berlin: Malik-Verlag, 1921.

Mit Pinsel und Schere: 7 Materialisationen. Monochrome reproduction after watercolor collages. Berlin: Malik-Verlag, 1922.

Die Räuber: Neun Lithographien zu Sentenzen aus Schillers Die Räuber. 9 lithographs. Berlin: Malik-Verlag, 1922.

Abrechnung folgt! 57 political drawings. Berlin: Malik-Verlag, 1923 (Kleine revolutinäre Bibliothek, 10).

Ecce Homo. 84 drawings, 16 watercolors. Berlin: Malik-Verlag, 1923.

Der Spiesser-Spiegel: 60 Berliner Bilder nach Zeichnungen mit einere Selbstdarstellung des Künstlers. Dresden: Carl Reissner Verlag, 1925.

Hintergrund: 17 Zeichnungen zur Aufführung des Schwejk *in der Piscator Bühne.* 17 hand-printed drawings. Berlin: Malik-Verlag, 1928.

Die Gezeichneten: 60 Blätter aus 15 Jahren. Berlin: Malik-Verlag, 1930.

Das neue Gesicht der herrschenden Klasse: 60 neue Zeichnungen. Berlin: Malik-Verlag, 1930.

Über alles die Liebe: 60 neue Zeichnungen. Berlin: Bruno Cassirer Verlag, 1930.

"Ade, Witboi": Mit 65 schwarzen und 20 farbigen unveröffentlichten Zeichnungen. 51 plates (4 in color), 14 text illustrations. Berlin: Arani Verlags-GmbH., 1955 (Introduction by Walter G. Oschilewski, postscript by C.W.O. Schmalhausen).

A Little Yes and a Big No: The Autobiography of George Grosz. Translated by Lola Sachs Dorin. New York: The Dial Press, 1946.

Ein kleines Ja und ein grosses Nein: Sein Leben von ihm selbst erzählt. Hamburg: Rowohlt Taschenbuch Verlag GmbH., 1976 (rororo 1759).

BIOGRAPHY

1893   George Grosz (Georg Gross) born on July 26 in Berlin as the third child of Karl and Marie (Schultze) Gross.

1898   Moves to Stolp, Pomerania with his parents.

1900   After the death of his father, moves to Berlin with his mother and sisters.

1902   Returns to Stolp with his family; attends grammar school; takes drawing lessons.

1908   Because of rebellious behavior he is expelled from school. Prepares for the entrance examination to the Royal Academy of Fine Arts, Dresden.

1909   Moves to Dresden and spends the following two years at the Academy.

1910   Publishes his first drawing in *Ulk*, a supplement of the *Berliner Tageblatt*.

1911   Graduates from the Academy.

1912   Settles in Berlin; lives first in the suburb of Charlottenburg, then in Südende. Enters the Art School of the Museum of Arts and Crafts and studies there until 1917. Works on book illustrations and starts painting in oil.

1913   First trip to Paris; studies at Atelier of Colarossi. Meeting with the painter Jules Pascin (1885–1930). Sells drawings to magazines (*Ulk* and *Lustige Blätter*).

1914   Enters military service as a volunteer and is discharged early 1915 after illness.

1915   Meets Wieland Herzfelde; publishes first poem and drawing in the magazine *Die Aktion*.

1916   He is active in Berlin; works for the magazine *Die Neue Jugend*, edited by Wieland Herzenfelde. Because of his enthusiasm for America changes his first name from Georg to George and his family name from Gross to Grosz.

1917   Drafted into the army, hospitalized after an illness, and then released from military service. Publication of first portfolio; works for Herzfelde's publishing house Malik-Verlag; meets Eva Louise Peter.

1918   Collaborates on an animated film with the artist John Heartfield, brother of Wieland Herzfelde; joins the Communist Party of Germany with John Heartfield, Wieland Herzfelde, and Erwin Piscator.

1919   Member of Berlin *Club Dada*; works on periodicals and books for Malik-Verlag. Makes Dada collages, partly in collaboration with John Heartfield.

1920   First one-man show at the gallery of Hans Goltz in Munich. Marries Eva Louise Peter. Exhibits at the first international Dada Fair. Designs his first sets and costumes (together with Heartfield) for Shaw's *Caesar and Cleopatra*, directed by Max Reinhardt. Grosz continues to design for the theater until 1930.

1921   Creates political drawings for periodicals, book illustrations, and portfolios. Tried, convicted, and fined for attacking the Reichswehr in his portfolio "Gott mit uns."

1922   Visits the Soviet Union for six months.

1923   Publication of portfolio "Ecco Homo" which is confiscated for offending public morals. Alfred Flechtheim becomes Grosz's dealer and he has his first show in Berlin. Leaves the German Communist Party (according to a later statement given to the FBI during the McCarthy investigations).

1924   Tried and fined for obscenity and the offending plates are removed from "Ecco Homo." Contributes to the communist satirical weekly, *Der Knüppel*, until 1927. Travels to Paris, and has his first exhibition there in November.

1925   Remains in France until October. His works are included at the *Neue Sachlichkeit* exhibition in Mannheim.

1926   His son, Peter Michael, is born.

1927   In the spring trip to Pointe Rouge, near Marseilles; returns to Berlin in the fall. He creates background drawings and stage effects for Erwin Piscator's production of *Schwejk*.

1928   Publication of portfolio "Hintergrund," followed by a trial for blasphemy that lasts until 1931. As a result one of the incriminatory drawings, "Christ with a Gas Mask," was to be destroyed.

1930   His second son, Martin Oliver, is born.

1931   Awarded Watson F. Blair Purchase Prize, Art Institute of Chicago. First one-man show in the U.S. at the Weyhe Gallery, New York.

1932   Guest lecturer at the Art Students League, New York from June to October; returns to Berlin.

1933   Emigrates to the U.S. with his family and settles in Bayside, Long Island. In Germany his work is labeled 'degenerate.' Together with Maurice Sterne starts his own art school in New York. Grosz also teaches periodically at the Art Students League until the late 1950's. In addition contributes illustrations to American magazines.

1938   Becomes American citizen.

While in the U.S. continues to produce—among many other works—political and anti-fascist drawings. At the same time, however, he becomes increasingly captivated by his new surroundings, and there are a large number of drawings and sketches that chronicle the American scene.

After the end of the war, and under the impact of the first atomic bomb, creates a series of so-called "stick men" drawings and watercolors that express a feeling of hopelessness.

1946   Publication of Grosz's autobiography *A Little Yes and a Big No* in New York.

1951   Visits Europe (France, Holland, Belgium, Italy, Switzerland, Monte Carlo).

1954   First trip to Germany since emigration.

1955   German edition of his autobiography is published.

1958   Spends two months in Berlin. Elected a member of the Akademie der Künste (Academy of Art), West Berlin.

1959   Final return to Berlin. Dies a few months later on July 6th.

SELECT BIBLIOGRAPHY

Anders, Günther. *George Grosz*. Zürich: Verlag Die Arche, 1961.

Bittner, Herbert (Ed.). *George Grosz*. Köln: DuMont Schauberg, 1961 (Introduction by Ruth Berenson and Norbert Mühlen. Includes Grosz-text "Über meine Zeichnungen").

Dückers, Alexander. *George Grosz: Das druckgraphische Werk*. Frankfurt: Propyläen Verlag, 1979.

Everett, Susanne. *Lost Berlin*. Chicago: Contemporary Books, Inc., 1979.

George Grosz: Retrospective Exhibition. Exhibition catalogue New York: Forum Gallery and E.V. Thaw & Co., 1963 (Introduction by Hans Hess).

George Grosz. Exhibition catalogue Wien: Graphische Sammlung Albertina, Linz: Neue Galerie der Stadt Linz Wolfgang Gurlitt Museum, Graz: Neue Galerie am Landesmuseum Joanneum, 1965 (Contributions by Walter Koschatzky, Walter Kasten and Erwin Piscator).

George Grosz: Dessins et Aquarelles. Exhibition catalogue Paris: Galerie Claude Bernard, 1966 (Introduction by Edouard Roditi).

George Grosz: A Selection of Fifty Early Drawings from 1910 to 1920. Exhibition catalogue New York: Peter Deitsch Fine Arts Inc., 1968.

George Grosz/John Heartfield. Exhibition catalogue Stuttgart: Württembergischer Kunstverein, 1969 (Introduction by Uwe M. Schneede and with texts by George Grosz, Max Herrmann-Neisse, Walter Mehring, Kurt Tucholsky, and others).

George Grosz: Berlin Drawings and Watercolors. Exhibition catalogue New York: Peter Deitsch Fine Arts Inc., 1970 (Introduction by Eila Kokkinen).

George Grosz: Theatrical Drawings and Watercolors. Exhibition catalogue Harvard University: Busch-Reisinger Museum, 1973 (Contributions by Hedy B. Landman and Herbert Knust).

George Grosz. Exhibition catalogue Washington: Lunn Gallery/Graphics International Ltd., 1974.

George Grosz: Dessins et Aquarelles. Exhibition catalogue Paris: Galerie Octave Negru, 1976 (Introduction by Serge Sabarsky).

George Grosz: Works in Oil. Exhibition catalogue Huntington, NY: Heckscher Museum, 1977 (Text by Eva Ingersoll Gatling).

George Grosz. Exhibition catalogue München: Galerie Ilse Schweinsteiger, 1977 (Introduction by Serge Sabarsky).

George Grosz: Einhundert Zeichnungen und Aquarelle aus den Jahren 1912–1942. Exhibition catalogue Bremen: Galerie Rolf Ohse, 1978.

George Grosz: 100 kleine Zeichnungen. Exhibition catalogue München: Galerie Ilse Schweinsteiger, 1985 (Introduction Hans Kinkel).

Hess, Hans. *George Grosz*. New York: Macmillan Publishing Co., Inc., 1974.

Lang, Lothar (Ed.). *George Grosz: 7 farbige Reproduktionen, 9 einfarbige Tafeln*. Berlin: Henschelverlag, 1966 (Includes text by Grosz "Statt einer Biographie" from "Die Kunst ist in Gefahr," Berlin 1925).

Lang, Lothar (Ed.). *George Grosz*. Berlin: Eulenspiegel Verlag, 1979 (Klassiker der Karikatur, 19).

Lewis, Beth Irwin. *George Grosz: Art and Politics in the Weimar Republic*. Madison: The University of Wisconsin Press, 1971.

Schneede, Uwe M. *George Grosz, der Künstler in seiner Gesellschaft*. Köln: DuMont Schauberg, 1975.

Schneede, Uwe M. (Ed.). *George Grosz: Leben und Werk*. Stuttgart: Verlag Gerd Hatje, 1975 (Contributions by Georg Bussmann and Marina Schneede-Sczesny).

Schneede, Uwe M. (Ed.). *George Grosz: His life and work*. Translated by Susanne Flatauer. New York: Universe Books, 1979 (Contributions by Georg Bussmann and Marina Schneede-Sczesny).

Werner, Bruno E. *Die Zwanziger Jahre: Von Morgens bis Mitternachts*. München: F. Bruckmann KG, 1962.

Finito di stampare nel gennaio 1986
presso le Arti Grafiche Leva A & G di Sesto S. Giovanni (MI)
per conto delle Nuove Edizioni Gabriele Mazzotta srl